Praise for *Toxi*

"Mixing psychological insights with concrete advice, ⸺ a powerful manifesto for reclaiming the idea of productivity—tra⸺ ⸺ing it from something toxic to nourishing."

—**Cal Newport,** *New York Times* bestselling author
of *Slow Productivity* and *Deep Work*

"In *Toxic Productivity*, Israa Nasir reveals the dirty secret behind doing enough: 'enough' never comes. Combining brain science and data-driven studies with wisdom from the therapy room and poignant personal anecdotes, *Toxic Productivity* is for the chronically overcommitted, the compulsively overachieving, and the constantly self-critical."

—**Eve Rodsky,** *New York Times* bestselling author of *Fair Play*

"In *Toxic Productivity*, Israa Nasir delivers a powerful wake-up call for anyone caught in the relentless cycle of hustle culture. Nasir's wisdom helps readers identify the deep-seated beliefs driving their overwork and offers actionable strategies to reclaim their time, energy, and sense of self. It's an essential read for anyone ready to stop running on the hamster wheel of achievement and start living a life that truly matters. This book doesn't just challenge the norms; it revolutionizes the way we think about productivity and self-worth."

—**Sue Varma,** author of *Practical Optimism*

"Do you obsess over 'making the most' of your free time? Does resting stress you out? Do you struggle with prioritizing self-care? If so, *Toxic Productivity* is the book you need right now! Discover how to reject hustle culture's relentless demands, silence your inner critic, and reclaim productivity on your own terms."

—**Alison Seponara, MS, LPC,** @theanxietyhealer, author,
and co-host of *The Anxiety Chicks Podcast*

"Motion and progress are correlated, but imperfectly; it is easy to work very hard and stay in the same place. In this insightful look at why we attend so much to what we're doing instead of where it is taking us, Nasir reminds us of the importance of getting off the hedonic treadmill and making deliberate choices about where we spend our energy."

—**Matt Walleart,** author of *Start at the End*

"In *Toxic Productivity*, Israa Nasir shows how hustle culture has hijacked our ability to live meaningful, connected lives, and offers expert guidance for reclaiming our time. A must-read for overachievers, perfectionists, and up-and-comers everywhere."

—**Amanda E. White, LPC,** author of *Not Drinking Tonight* and founder of @therapyforwomen

"Israa Nasir has written a must-read primer for anyone that can do it all even though they know they shouldn't . . . this book will help them learn how to do what matters and take a step back from what doesn't."

—**Elizabeth Earnshaw, LMFT,** author of *'Til Stress Do Us Part*

"Today's pressures of having to do more leads us to keep striving and overachieving, resulting in increased rates of burnout. This book is for everyone who finds themselves wondering 'When will it feel like I've done enough?' Israa Nasir shows how to reimagine your relationship with productivity and reclaim your right to simply be."

—**Tracy Dalgleish, CPsych,** author of *I Didn't Sign Up for This*

"*Toxic Productivity* is essential reading for anybody who is feeling demoralized, burned out, or exhausted from trying to do their best or doing better than ever in their work life. Israa Nasir gives you her hard-earned wisdom about how to remain productive without letting that productivity become a nightmare for your wellbeing or the wellbeing of your family."

—**Corey Keyes,** author of *Languishing: How To Feel Alive Again In A World That Wears Us Down*

Productivity

Reclaim Your Time and
Emotional Energy in a World
That Always Demands *More*

Israa Nasir, MHC-LP

Bridge City Books

Published by
Bridge City Books, an imprint of PESI Publishing, Inc.
3839 White Ave
Eau Claire, WI 54703

Cover and interior design by Emily Dyer
Editing by Chelsea Thompson

Library of Congress Cataloging-in-Publication Data
Names: Nasir, Israa, author.
Title: Toxic productivity: reclaim your time and emotional energy in a
   world that always demands more / Israa Nasir, MHC-LP.
Description: Eau Claire, WI: Bridge City Books, [2024] | Includes
   bibliographical references. |
Identifiers: LCCN 2024036908 | ISBN 9781962305358 (print) | ISBN
   9781962305372 (ePUB | ISBN 9781962305389 (ePDF)
Subjects: LCSH: Self-esteem. | Burn out (Psychology) | Work-life balance. |
   Quality of life. | Labor productivity--Psychological aspects.
Classification: LCC BF697.5.S46 N37 2024 | DDC 158.1--dc23/eng
   /20240814
LC record available at https://lccn.loc.gov/2024036908

Bridge City Books

To Mama and Baba, for teaching me
lessons in love, optimism, and resilience.

"If you want to build a ship, don't drum up the
men to gather wood, divide the work, and give orders.
Instead, teach them to yearn for the vast and endless sea."

—Antoine de Saint-Exupéry

Table of Contents

Author's Note

As a therapist, I have had the privilege of working with many clients who have entrusted me with the story of their lives. In this book, I share a number of client stories to illustrate the concepts I am exploring. To protect the privacy of the individuals involved, these stories are composites, woven together from real-life challenges, lessons, and triumphs that a variety of clients have shared with me over the years. Though specific details and circumstances in these stories have been altered, the essence of each narrative remains rooted in the universal struggles and successes of the human experience.

Along with helping you reflect on the underlying themes and lessons in these stories, my hope is to demonstrate that personal development is both a universal experience and an individual journey. May the experiences of these individuals serve as inspiration and guidance on your own path toward a more fulfilling and empowered life.

With gratitude,

Israa

Introduction

"Exhaustion is a status symbol because we desperately
want to be seen, we desperately want to belong.
We want to believe we're lovable."

—Brené Brown

"I can't remember the last time I didn't feel tired."

A few years ago, this was probably the phrase I said most often. Looking back at myself at that time, I see someone pushing herself to keep doing more—someone who put everything into her work, while at the same time starting and scaling a passion project into a business; someone running from one social obligation to the other, eating protein bars on the way to parties because she worked through lunch; someone so obsessed with "being there" for her family and social circle that she kept saying yes to things, knowing full well she did not have capacity for them.

On the outside, I looked like someone that society would call successful: I was married, living in New York City, working in the rapidly rising field of digital health, going out to shows and plays in the evenings. Anyone would have assumed that I was thriving.

But on the inside, all I could think was, *You are not doing enough. You should have done more. Why aren't you doing as well as others? You don't deserve this rest.* The weight of these thoughts was an emotional burden I was carrying everywhere, making it more difficult to handle the tasks on my to-do list and offering me much less relaxation at the end of the day.

I couldn't separate the thoughts about myself from the things I did. The "do more to feel more" mentality permeated every aspect of my life, including how I spent my weekend mornings, how many books I was reading, and how dedicated I was to personal development. Regardless of how many speaking engagements I booked, articles I wrote, date nights I curated, or self-help content I consumed, it did not feel like enough. Soon, I realized that my sense of identity had become dependent on my productivity.

I noticed that although I was busy *all* the time, I wasn't feeling much fulfillment from doing these things. In fact, I was feeling empty. Instead of feeling proud of the task I had just completed, I kept looking ahead to the next thing that would satisfy my expectations. I felt like I was missing one last check mark on my list, the one that would assure me that I had done enough—that I *was* enough.

If any of this sounds familiar, then you've come to the right place.

* * *

Think back to the last time you had a few hours of "empty" time on a weekend or an evening. Were you stressed at the prospect of not knowing what to do with your free time? Were you trying to find the perfect task or activity to fill that time? Do you remember any distinct emotions? Perhaps a nagging feeling of being "behind," despite not having a schedule to keep? Were your thoughts accusing you of being lazy or wasting time?

Maybe you find yourself in the middle of some "free time" right now, trying desperately not to waste a moment. Perhaps you've been combing through personal development sections in bookstores for the latest and greatest way to optimize your life. Maybe your Google searching is steering you more and more toward "how to be more productive" or "recovery from burnout." Or perhaps a loved one gave you this very book as a not-so-subtle hint. No matter how you got here, something about this book's title must have resonated or, at the very least, intrigued you.

Why Do We Push Ourselves to Do Better?

You may have heard the ancient Greek myth that tells the story of Sisyphus, a king who was banished by Hades and doomed to spend eternity rolling a boulder up a hill. Every time Sisyphus reached the top, the boulder would slip back down the hill, forcing him to start from the beginning all over again. Philosophers, poets, and artists have offered a variety of explanations for what this myth signifies, but my first thought upon reading it was, *Hmm—his eternal task kind of seems familiar.* Doing the same thing over and over again, getting tired but continuing nevertheless, finishing a task only to start a new one without ever being able to see or appreciate your progress. I could relate to Sisyphus—I'd been pushing myself for what seemed like an eternity. More importantly, I was starting to feel the immense strain from my own boulder weighing me down after all these years.

As a therapist, I'm trained to look at the "why" behind the "what." Since the quantity of my workload didn't seem to impact the quality of how I felt, I decided to look at my problem through the lens of behavioral psychology. I dove into the research on habit change, motivation, time management—all ingredients that play a role in how productive we are. I tested out a variety of techniques and theories on myself: habit stacking, the Eisenhower Matrix, and the Pomodoro Technique among others. While these strategies did help me feel more organized and in control of my time, they failed to change the way I saw myself in relation to others, the way I felt about my achievements, or the way I valued myself as a human. Whether I found myself with free time at the end of the day or passed out in bed with my laptop open in front of me, my inner critical voice continued to tell me that what I was doing was not enough.

It finally dawned on me that these weren't just fleeting thoughts or simple products of stress or desire. This was the voice of my *emotional foundation*. The emotional foundation is the underlying structure that defines both our internal and external worldview. Formed by our early experiences, temperament and personality, beliefs and value system, and emotional dynamics, it guides our thoughts, decisions, and habits.

Because the emotional foundation serves as the basis for how we move through the world, we tend to accept it as an unchangeable truth—*this is just who I am*. The truth is that the emotional foundation has parts that are learned, which means we can *unlearn* them. I had learned that my identity was based on my productivity, and until I examined this more closely, my inner critical voice wasn't going anywhere.

We develop our emotional foundation through early life experiences. Throughout childhood, the adults in our lives encourage us to mine our potential for all we can achieve. In college, our scope expands—we want to maximize our contribution to the world and make a difference for the better. But as some of us reach adulthood, these lofty goals tend to boil down to a single, urgent imperative: in order to have value, we have to produce more value. Without our noticing, our sense of self shifts away from our internal potential toward what that potential can produce: education, salary, material possessions, relationships, reputation. Our personal value is measured not by what we've produced already, but by how today's production can help us produce tomorrow. Add this together with our competitive results-driven world filled with messages to "rise and grind" or "go the extra mile" and it's no surprise that we are never satisfied.

This brings us to pursuing productivity relentlessly, to the point that we prioritize it over our physical, emotional, and mental health—in other words, we sometimes choose productivity over our basic human needs. Doing this builds habits like perfectionism, overcommitting, insecurity, self-neglect, and isolation. Even our proudest achievements cease to have any meaning for us; they're simply a row of checkmarks on a never-ending list, a line of stepping stones toward a destination we will never reach.

This is what I call *toxic productivity*.

What's Wrong with Wanting to Do Better?

One day at brunch, a friend and I were discussing the pros and cons of listening to podcasts.

"Sometimes I try to listen when I cook, but it's too distracting," I told him.

"And I can't listen at the gym," he replied. "It just doesn't work for me; I can't focus."

"Yeah, and then I fall behind on so many good episodes."

We both munched our french fries morosely, contemplating our problem.

Suddenly, he had an epiphany. "Israa, why do we have to listen to podcasts at all, if it's stressing us out so much?"

A little taken aback, I looked at him like he had asked a silly question.

"Well, because there are so many good podcasts coming out. I'll feel like I'm wasting my time if I don't use it for my growth! What's wrong with that?" He paused, wondering the same.

This mindset, in a nutshell, is the toxic productivity mindset. We believe that productivity, no matter the cost, is never a bad thing—in fact, it's a good, valuable thing.

However, before we get into the details, I want to clarify that I'm not advocating that we abandon all notions of productivity entirely. The antidote to toxic productivity is not the absence of productivity. Instead, I'm calling for a radical reimagining of what productivity means. To be productive is to put your goals and habits in service of your emotional and personal growth, not in service of a checklist that is rooted in comparison, shame, or perfectionism.

Healthy productivity is seeing the difference between urgent things and important things; feeling empowered to say no, or at least "not so much" or "not this time"; and having balance and flexibility instead of being hyper-focused on one outcome. I see healthy productivity as being more sustainable because it includes guardrails that help you stay connected to your values and goals over a long period of time, without sacrificing your health and wellness.

Maybe you're thinking, *Why should I make a change? I'm perfectly happy with the fact that I can get things done and move ahead in life, even when I feel stressed about it.* It's a fair question. I've had many clients share the same sort of skepticism about the idea that becoming less productive will make them feel happier and more positive about themselves.

The reason this concept seems so foreign is because most of us are taught to live in binaries. It is much easier to reason and identify with issues when they are either A or B, black or white. From contemporary political parties to using a Mac or PC, we're either one thing or the other. Therefore, in the world of productivity, it might seem like there are only two options: we are productive, or we are lazy, unambitious, and willing to settle for less. And if this is the case, when we're not doing something worthwhile, we are automatically part of the dreaded "other half."

But being productive is not, in and of itself, a toxic action. In fact, productivity is the driving force in achieving goals and simply getting things done. This is why it's so important to shift your mindset from *toxic* productivity to *healthy* productivity. Through the information, reflections, and exercises in this book, you will learn to identify the connection between productivity and self-worth, learn more about the subtle ways it can show up in your life, and reimagine your own relationship with productivity.

How to Use This Book

This book is the result of my research as both a therapist and a human being, but it is also the outcome of my effort to decouple *what I do* from *who I am*. My hope is that it can help you do the same. This book will explore what underlying factors drive toxic productivity in your life and offer simple strategies you can integrate into your daily life for overcoming it. Every chapter includes exercises that will help you recognize red flags, identify underlying emotional motivators, and work through your triggers. There will also be reflection prompts and questions to help you consider how you spend your time, how you feel about yourself and your achievements, and what thoughts and emotions come up for you when you are not busy. If something doesn't apply to you or doesn't resonate, that simply means that it doesn't fit your specific situation or needs. Feel free to tweak any of the strategies or reflections to make them work better for you. I encourage you to write in the book itself or to have a journal or digital diary to write out your responses to the reflection exercises, as well as any insights or feelings that might come up for you.

The last suggestion I will offer, which has helped me when I try to incorporate a new habit to my routine, is to take an "80/20" approach to it. This means that I am flexible with myself about integrating new habits into my life and begin with aiming for an 80 percent success or completion rate. If you can't commit to doing something every day, aim to do it for three days out of the week. If you can't practice a habit or reflection for 30 minutes, do it for 15 minutes. Starting small and slow helps make a new habit into a practiced skill. And in case it needs to be said, there is no pressure to finish this book in one sitting or even in the same month. Some of these reflections might bring up intense emotions or cover things you don't want to think about. That's okay. Be gentle with yourself. Give yourself the grace and space to meet yourself where you are at, to be slow and intentional with your changes, and ultimately, to build a life that you are in love with.

Since understanding ourselves better is the first step in making healthy long-term habits, my purpose for writing this book is to empower you with deeper self-awareness that strengthens the relationship you have with yourself, allowing you to understand, manage, and ultimately shift the intense emotions related to achievements and self-worth.

I hope that after reading this book, you feel more confident in building a newer, healthier relationship with productivity, and live a more joyful life.

Exercise

Setting an Intention

Before we dive into this work together, I want to invite you to set an intention. Setting an intention before starting something new helps you stay grounded when things get tough or when plans get derailed (as they often do!). Think of your intention as the destination address you put into your GPS, and your goals as the step-by-step directions you take to get there.

For this exercise, think about why you chose to read this book. Consider what type of thoughts and feelings led you to choose a book about toxic productivity. Are there any parts of your life you want to change or any new habits that you're hoping to implement as you read this book?

Exercise

Keep, Stop, Start

Reflect on your current productivity habits with the following questions. What will the next 30 days look like for you?

1. **Keep:** What do you want to *keep* doing in the next 30 days?

2. **Start:** What do you want to *start* doing in the next 30 days that you are not doing right now?

3. **Stop:** What do you want to *stop* doing in the next 30 days?

Chapter 1

What Is Toxic Productivity?

"Measure your worth by your dedication to
your path, not by your successes and failures."

—Elizabeth Gilbert, *Big Magic*

A few years ago, my friend and I were browsing the aisles in a New York City bookshop when she stopped at the fiction section.

Without thinking, I said, "I haven't read any new fiction books lately," as I moved past her toward the personal development section.

She grabbed my arm and nudged me back toward the fiction aisle. "Israa, if you haven't read any fiction lately, why don't you get this new Sally Rooney one? Everyone is talking about it."

I hesitated, thinking instead about the latest productivity book I had heard about, *Four Thousand Weeks* by Oliver Burkeman. Before I could open my mouth, she had already pushed the Sally Rooney hardcover into my hands.

"I can't just sit for four hours and read a random novel," I protested. "I literally have no time and so much to do. Plus, I just read a review of *Four Thousand Weeks* and I know it'll be helpful for me right now. Sally Rooney isn't going anywhere. I feel like my time would be better used if I read for my own growth."

This sentiment is the essence of toxic productivity. It speaks to a mindset obsessed with "hyper-optimization"—trying to make the most of every waking hour by working toward outcomes, achievement, and productivity.

My friend looked at me incredulously. "Are you hearing yourself? All the articles you send me and the books on your shelf are about personal growth these days." She paused for a breath. "You know, you don't need to be learning *all* the time."

Later that evening, I couldn't stop thinking about what my friend had said. I used to enjoy reading, fiction included. Now I couldn't remember the last time I read something for fun. Somewhere along the way, almost without my noticing, reading had become something I solely used for personal development—to learn about myself, to better myself, and to make sure I was up to date with current topics in the field of self-improvement.

I wondered what else in my life I had begun doing exclusively for personal growth. So, I took out my journal and listed all the opportunities and habits I had taken on in the last year in the name of growing as a person. I reflected on whether these activities were something I truly wanted to do or merely things I felt I *should* be doing.

Here's what I found:

- I was no longer reading for pleasure, but for learning instead.

- When I sat down to watch a movie, it had to be "serious" and teach me something.

- I had channeled my passion for writing into a monthly newsletter that I was no longer enjoying writing.

- I was forcing myself to wake up extra early to accomplish a series of "self-care" tasks (eat breakfast, work out, journal, meditate) before starting work, but these tasks weren't really making me feel good. In fact, I was slogging through journaling and meditation just to check them off my list.

This reflection was the very beginning of an inward exploration that led to recognizing and unlearning the toxic productivity messages I had learned throughout my life.

What Is Toxic Productivity?

The term *toxic* can be used to describe habits or behaviors that have crossed a threshold of intensity or frequency that makes them unhealthy. In other words, it is taking a generally helpful action to an extreme where it causes more harm than good. For example, doing a favor for a loved one or being positive can both be healthy, good habits. But when doing favors turns into chronic people-pleasing, or putting a smile on turns into masking your true feelings, the behaviors may now be toxic.

In the case of toxic productivity, unhealthy habits begin to show when we consistently put work, personal development, or accomplishment above our personal needs. Some examples of toxic habits are:

- Turning down social events to do work or self-improvement
- Forgetting (or choosing not) to eat meals during the day
- Feeling guilty about not getting enough done
- Working overtime on a regular basis
- Feeling overwhelmed with events or activities for weeks (or months) at a time

However, recall that we are used to thinking in binaries, so it's likely we see an action as A) healthy or B) toxic. But a productivity binary, much like many other binaries, is a false construct. There is no A *or* B—black *or* white, healthy *or* toxic; instead, productivity lives on a spectrum. You can be productive *and* go out with friends after work (instead of it being a waste of time). You can get things done *and* choose not to follow culturally prescribed goals (instead of being unambitious). In fact, the power of being "somewhere in between" is where we have the most flexibility to grow, to find our sweet spot, and to have compassion for ourselves and others.

However, as we move toward the toxic end of the spectrum, we begin to feel a negative impact on our overall health. This impact can happen in two ways. Toxic productivity habits negatively affect our physical health, as the desire to be productive outweighs our priority for sleeping, eating a consistently healthy diet, or making time for social relationships. Remaining in the more extreme end of the spectrum can also impact us at the emotional level, causing us to feel self-doubt, inviting comparison of ourselves to others, and amplifying shame and guilt. These habits strengthen feelings of low self-worth and the lack of belonging. At the most extreme, we can experience *burnout*—a feeling of profound emotional, physical, and mental exhaustion as a result of excessive and prolonged stress.[1]

Unfortunately, it is very easy to overlook these feelings as we chase the high of meeting a goal or achieving something. The more we ignore this emotional distress, the more it starts to show up in our relationships as irritability and short tempers, our bodies as vague aches and fatigue, and our minds as cynicism and pessimism. We can even become "stuck" in our toxic productivity, where our own thoughts and behaviors fuel even more negative thoughts and behaviors, pushing us further toward the toxic end of the spectrum.

How Do You Know If You're Stuck in Toxic Productivity?

In David Foster Wallace's 2005 commencement speech at Kenyon College (later published as an essay titled "This Is Water"), he tells a story about two young fish who are swimming in a lake.[2] An older fish swims by and asks, "How's the water, boys?" After the older fish swims away, the two younger fish look at each other and wonder, "What the hell is water?"

Wallace's story points out that when we are surrounded by something, it becomes difficult to recognize it. We live in a world immersed in messages that glorify toxic productivity, such as aspirational phrases like "hustle culture" or "boss energy"; these messages make it difficult to even notice, let alone discern, which parts of their impact are healthy or unhealthy for you.

Learning to objectively observe yourself is one of the most important ways you can become aware of your toxic thoughts and behaviors, break the toxic productivity cycle, and begin to heal yourself. In fact, self-awareness is a key first step in changing *any* behavior. Ask yourself where you currently fall on the productivity spectrum: see if your thoughts and behaviors could be classified as normal productive actions or if they are becoming too toxic—causing more harm than good. The following lists are some of the most common thoughts or statements clients have shared with me that reflect their toxic productivity mindset. Take a look and reflect on whether you've ever caught yourself saying or thinking anything similar:

- "I'll take on this project as well. Really, it's no problem."
- "You go ahead—I'll eat lunch later."

- "I'm leaving for vacation tomorrow, but I'll still have access to my work email, so don't hesitate to reach out if anything comes up."

- "I'll sleep better after I've finished _____."

- "If they were truly my friends, they'd understand why I can't get together on weeknights."

- "I can't delegate this task! No one can do this as perfectly as I can."

Once you are more aware of your toxic productivity thoughts and habits, you can ponder the why behind the what—looking into your thoughts regarding productivity in general and how these affect your thoughts and behaviors. You can use this information to finally see all the "water" that surrounds you.

The Toxic Productivity Mindset

Have you ever spent more time worrying about the tasks on your to-do list than actually working on those tasks? It's not because you don't know how to do the tasks, but because you feel frozen by indecision about where to begin. Perhaps you get started on one task, but anxious thoughts about the rest of the list make it difficult for you to focus, causing you to spend more time on the task than it normally takes. To avoid this problem, you might plan out how to tackle your tasks, organizing your folders or notes or ranking your list in an order that makes sense. This, however, leads to more or less the same problem: spending more time thinking about your work than actually doing the work. All the while, your mind keeps reminding you of the things you *could* and *should* be doing. Eventually, this internal power struggle saps your motivation. Exhausted and overwhelmed, you simply give up, putting aside your to-do list until tomorrow, when it will inevitably grow longer, and the cycle repeats. Sound familiar?

This problem, commonly known as "analysis paralysis," arises when the desire to be productive is so strong that it gets in the way of being productive. This deadlock triggers anxiety and self-doubt, feeding into your sense of being "behind." And what seems to be the only cure for this feeling? You guessed it: being more productive. This is how we find ourselves stuck in an infinite self-defeating loop of stress and overwhelm—the toxic productivity mindset.

It's easy to stay stuck in the toxic productivity mindset because the mental and emotional energy that it expends gives you a false sense of having done something. And, indeed, you've done work in some form: you've spent time thinking about the tasks on your to-do list, preparing to do the tasks, and managing your experience of stress related to the tasks. The problem is that the work you've done isn't the work that you set out to do. You've stayed busy, but the to-do list remains untouched.

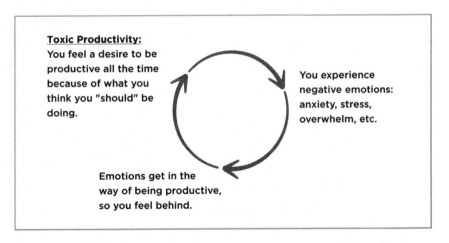

Toxic Productivity:
You feel a desire to be productive all the time because of what you think you "should" be doing.

You experience negative emotions: anxiety, stress, overwhelm, etc.

Emotions get in the way of being productive, so you feel behind.

In addition, the toxic mindset creates an environment of self-judgment in your mind, keeping you focused on what you haven't done instead of acknowledging the things you have done. This feeling of failure can send your anxiety and stress into overdrive, making it even more likely that you will miss deadlines, overcommit yourself, and work on tasks for much longer than they should require. Naturally, this primes you for further failure. Thus, you remain stuck in the loop of toxic productivity: feeling behind, stressing out to catch up and get ahead, getting overwhelmed, freezing up, and finally falling (or feeling) behind all over again.

Toxic? Definitely. Intentional? Not quite. Many of us don't have the awareness of how we perpetuate toxic productivity in our lives. The work of healing begins with building awareness of behavior patterns; we will discuss these patterns and how to recognize them in chapter 2.

What Fuels Toxic Productivity?

Let's consider that elusive final check mark on your to-do list to be your end goal. You know that you must do *more* to get there. However, the steps you are taking toward fulfillment are getting you no closer, and it is beginning to affect your health and your emotional state. Still you soldier on. But if you continue to pack your schedule and stay busy despite the lack of satisfaction—if, in fact, these actions are actually holding you back—then there has to be something deeper at work. To find out why you maintain these unhealthy behaviors, you must ask yourself, *What is this toxic productivity really offering me?*

To figure out the hidden "promise" behind your toxic behaviors, it's important to recognize the emotional dynamics that are running the show. Three major subconscious motivators of toxic productivity are:

1. **Shaming yourself for not being good enough, smart enough, fast enough, or simply *enough*:** Your habits are an effort to make up for what you believe you lack.

2. **Being a perfectionist in how you meet others' expectations, or even your own expectations for yourself:** Your habits are an effort to maintain a rigid ideal of what you "should" be.

3. **Comparing yourself to others or to an idealized version of yourself:** Your habits are an effort to win others' approval or to deserve the success you admire in someone else.

Though productivity has the ability to make us happy if we enjoy our work or believe in the positive impact it can have, there is a problem when we rely on productivity for happiness at a more foundational level—a bid for acceptance, respect, a sense of purpose, belonging, or self-worth. This, I believe, is the root of why we pursue productivity so relentlessly. This is also why merely using time management or organizational hacks cannot solve our productivity problems. To break out of the toxic mindset, we must heal the emotional patterns that sustain it—starting from the strong messages we received about productivity, belonging, and self-worth in early childhood.

Where Do Our Beliefs Come From?

Stories have always interested me. As a young child, I spent many hours absorbed in reading stories or making up my own. This has made my job as a therapist not only easier but incredibly gratifying, as each client entrusts me with their own story. Inside every client that comes into my office is a unique narrative, held together by their perspective on the events and experiences in their life, their emotional inheritance (the patterns, habits, and coping skills passed down from the people who raised them), and the conclusions they have drawn about their personal identity and value. Telling stories is the way we make sense of the world around us and our own place in it. My work is to help clients discover and examine the stories they believe about themselves and, where necessary, rewrite these stories. This rewriting phase is where we empower ourselves to make the changes we seek.

Our stories tend to start with messages we have learned during childhood. Whether it be a lesson from a caretaker (usually parents, but can include extended family, teachers, siblings, peers, etc.), a part of our cultural or spiritual upbringing, or a major life experience that left us with a startling conclusion, these stories become the blueprint for how we view the world and ourselves. In other words, they become our beliefs.

"Are you going to tell me all the ways my parents messed me up?" is a question I am asked often. It's almost always said in a playful, half-joking way. However, there is a truth there; we are significantly impacted by our early childhood experiences. Of course, the intent of therapy is not to trash your parents and absolve you of all responsibility. No, the intent of digging into your early years is to become more aware of your inner workings, the foundation of your interactions with the world and your life. Once you gain this awareness, you can more easily identify harmful or unhelpful lessons learned from childhood experiences and work to unlearn them, creating space for new ways of engaging with your emotions, relationships, and your life. In short, this is how you rewrite your story—this is how you grow.

So, how do your original caretakers impact your relationship with productivity? I'll explain this in a story about my client, Margaret.

Margaret, a woman in her late thirties, started working with me to overcome the feeling of, in her words, not being "good enough." After years of doing more than she could handle to show her commitment to her job, she was suddenly having trouble feeling connected to the organization or to her role in it. This sudden drop in motivation left her feeling apathetic and lethargic. She started having anxious thoughts that this attitude would lead to a critical mistake that would put her livelihood in jeopardy. She also wondered if this feeling was transitioning into her personal relationships as well.

"I mean, I know that the people in my life—my husband Brian, friends, coworkers—care about me," Margaret said. "But I feel the same disconnection with them that I have at work." Reaching for a tissue, she abruptly asked, "Can you feel lonely in a good relationship?"

"Yes, of course—loneliness and being alone are different things," I said, offering validation to her difficult feelings. "Last week, we discussed your feelings about how you and Brian spend time together. You mentioned that you're feeling hesitant to tell him that you want to go out more and not watch as much TV together as a couple. What are some thoughts you have when you consider telling him?"

"That he'll think I'm difficult or being picky . . ." She sighed. "He's not like that, I know. But I don't want to impose myself on him or how he spends his evenings after work." She paused. "I know I'm not centering myself; I'm centering him and his needs. I just . . . I want him to be happy being with me," she said quickly.

"What do you think makes you feel lonely?" I asked, in an attempt to string the two thoughts into one.

"I guess I feel like Brian doesn't *get* me, and it makes me feel disconnected from him. I don't understand why . . ." She trailed off, shifting in her chair.

"Go on, it's okay—this is your space," I encouraged.

At that, she burst into tears. "That's exactly the problem. I don't understand why I just don't take space anywhere! I'm always holding myself back. I know I have more to offer and say, but . . . I just don't do it."

After giving her a few minutes to cry it out (we all need it sometimes!), I asked her, "Is there a story or belief you have about why people make space for you in their lives?"

Over that session and in future sessions, Margaret uncovered deeply hidden stories she believed about herself and her value in relationships, both personal and professional, as we explored her early childhood experiences and her relationships with parents and siblings. Margaret grew up with a passive father who gave her limited guidance on what healthy achievements looked like, and a highly demanding but rejecting mother who offered little beyond criticism and emotional distance. Margaret learned early on that "being good" was the only way to connect with her parents. Specifically, she internalized that a certain type of physical appearance, a high standard of academic performance, polite behavior, and most of all, never stating her own opinions, were ways to win attention, acceptance, and validation.

Through examining the stories she had hidden away, Margaret realized that her belief about her relationships was, *People will make space for me only when I am good.* This belief, which formed in childhood and continued into adulthood, is what we call a *core belief.* Core beliefs are general principles—positive, neutral, or negative in nature—that we have adopted about ourselves (internal) and the world (external). We will discuss the nuances of core beliefs more in chapter 3, but know that these beliefs have an extremely strong influence on our thoughts, actions, and relationships.[3, 4]

In Margaret's case, the dynamic she had with her mother had taught her that she was not worthy of love for its own sake, that people will value her only when she is productive. As an adult, she was unknowingly replicating this belief at work and in her relationships, especially with her husband. Naturally, this made her feel unseen, disconnected, and lonely.

Becoming curious about your childhood experiences and trying to figure out what they've taught you is a compelling way to learn how you can manage them. Echoes of old feelings like loneliness, resentment, and guilt are painful to experience, but they are also messengers that help us recognize that something is off in how we understand love, achievement, and our own self-worth.

Exercise

Lessons from Childhood

One way to unlearn the lessons from childhood is to become aware of what you still believe and carry into your current relationships. Use the following questions to reflect on your past experiences:

1. What stories do you believe about what makes you "good"? Which parts of this story can be traced back to your caregivers' messages about achievement, approval, and love?

2. Where in your life today are you replicating these stories?

3. Now that you know this, how do you feel? Where do these feelings show up in your body? What thoughts come up for you?

4. What are a few ways you can shift your perception or behavior to break this pattern? (You don't have to take any action right away—for now, just think about it.)

It can't be denied that healing is heavy work. If you relate to any of this, the previous section and exercise might have been very difficult. I encourage you to pause and take a breath. Maybe put the book down and get a glass of water.

Another way to stay grounded if you're feeling activated is to turn your attention toward your body. If you can and feel called, do an intentional body scan. Sit in a comfortable position and take a deep inhale for three counts, then exhale for three counts. Finally, put all your attention toward your toes and imagine releasing any tension. Then work upward—your calves, your thighs, and so on—until you get to the top of your head. Remember to deeply inhale and exhale as you do this.

If you are someone who has a hard time with stillness in times of emotional distress, I encourage you to regulate your emotions through movement (dancing, going for a walk, etc.) or taking a cold shower. You can also take a break from heavy emotions by watching a relaxing movie or TV show, or reaching out to a trusted, safe person.

Healing Begins with Awareness

We must be *aware* before we can initiate change. Recall that the first step in stopping our toxic productivity thoughts and habits is to objectively observe and become aware of them. Similarly, we must first bring awareness to what we believe before we can begin to unlearn it.

Once we develop a belief system, we typically live within the framework of the belief without questioning it; in other words, our thoughts become truths. Therefore, when you bring your "truth" to the forefront by gaining more awareness, it will likely feel overwhelming, to the point that you might want to walk away from it. Feeling overwhelmed is a normal part of the healing process, as you are intentionally shifting your focus to things that you usually don't think about, have been ignoring, or have even repressed for a long time. Once you increase this self-awareness, it can feel at first like everything is "wrong." This is because awareness changes the way you view the world. Change is scary, even when it is a positive change, because on the other side of change lies the unknown.

This sense of overwhelm can also make you impatient—restless for the change to happen now. After the first burst of relief following a breakthrough in self-awareness, it's not uncommon for my clients to start asking, "Okay—now what?" or "I know all this stuff now, but nothing feels different."

But things don't change just because we know about them. Healing comes from self-awareness, self-reflection, and intentional action. Keep in mind that you are not finding reasons to judge or shame yourself, nor are you taking responsibility for issues that are outside your control. Rather, healing takes place when you develop curiosity; consciously look inward; reflect on the way you think, feel and act; and then make the choice to change how you think, feel, and act.

Later in the book, we will take an in-depth look at the specific motivations that underlie toxic productivity habits, and you will get a chance to explore your own why. For now, I'll leave you to reflect on this question: what might happiness look like for you, in the absence of being productive?

Key Takeaways

- There is a healthy approach to productivity and an unhealthy (toxic) approach to productivity; most habits *can* be healthy, but they become toxic when they cause more harm than good.

- Different types of emotional dynamics can keep us stuck in the toxic productivity mindset: shame, perfectionism, and comparison. (We will explore each of these dynamics in later chapters.)

- We learn harmful or unhelpful messages about productivity through early childhood experiences, and we must work to be aware of them and unlearn them.

- To break out of toxic productivity, we must understand the why behind our productivity habits (what fuels our attitude and actions in getting things done).

Chapter 2

How Does Toxic Productivity Show Up in Your Life?

"He does not seem to me to be a free man
who does not sometimes do nothing."

—Marcus Tullius Cicero, *letters to Quintus and Brutus*

A few years ago, I was working at a rapidly growing mental health start-up staffed by just a handful of people. We were facing an increasing demand for virtual therapy services from clients, which meant days overloaded with multiple meetings, three to four deliverables due at any given time, and video calls fraught with technical issues.

On top of all this, I had decided to launch a digital wellness platform at that time. (I know, I know.) This meant that instead of unplugging and unwinding at the end of a stressful workday, I spent my evenings designing creative content for mental health education. I distinctly remember a two-week period when I was extremely sick but convinced myself to keep working through the first week of it. I even hosted a live virtual talk because I felt like I couldn't reschedule it. The second week, I finally took time off work, but only because I naively thought it would be the perfect opportunity to write and pitch articles to media publications. (It was not.)

Even as I write this, I am embarrassed by my lack of self-awareness at that time. But the story does illustrate the point we touched on in the previous chapter: self-awareness is a key component in managing toxic productivity. After all, you can't manage something that you don't know exists.

Toxic Productivity and Your Values

Toxic productivity is driven by a desire for belonging, and we erroneously believe that by achieving certain milestones, we will gain a sense of validation and acceptance from others. Our toxic habits are not really a way to get things done, but rather a way to cope with uncomfortable feelings about our own sense of worth. In this chapter, we will explore how you can identify toxic patterns in your life and understand how these patterns affect you. Let's start by looking at my client, Maya.

Maya was a woman whose idea of success was tied to meeting the timelines of society. Everything had to happen by a specific time in her life: finishing school and postgraduate studies, climbing the corporate ladder at a steady pace, being married with children, buying property, and traveling to hand-picked locations to have specific experiences.

At 39, Maya felt like she had somehow fallen behind because she was single, still rented an apartment, and felt stuck in her job. Her life was not objectively bad—she loved her apartment, valued her coworkers, and enjoyed spending time with her friends. She found these achievements rewarding, but they didn't meet her mental checklist, especially when compared to her peers and the people she followed online. It was difficult for her to appreciate her own efforts and accomplishments, and her self-judgment kept her in a state of constant overwhelm. Maya even felt like she was running out of time to hit her milestones, so she found herself working overtime and taking on too much; in her mind, she could get closer to reaching her goals if she did as much as she was possibly capable of.

"Maya, you mentioned that you feel unhappy because you haven't hit the milestones you should have by now. I'm wondering what these milestones represent for you?" I asked.

"Success, probably. That I have my life together. That I'm . . . as good as everyone else, I guess, if I check all the boxes," she said quietly.

I know this checklist mindset all too well. I grew up in a household that required me to be a good daughter (check), an attentive sister (check), and an A+ student (check), not to mention excel at a wide variety of extracurricular activities (check, check, check). Like Maya, how I felt about myself became directly connected to what I did, cementing an emotional relationship between productivity and self-worth.

"It's not uncommon to use societal expectations as a measuring stick for your own success," I reassured her. "It's something many of us, me included, have struggled with at some point in our lives. There is a risk, though, of becoming disconnected with yourself and your values when you chase what others value."

I let her consider this idea before asking a question that had helped me get out of the checklist mindset: "If you had to focus on accomplishing the things that make you feel good, what would those things be?"

"I haven't really thought that much about that," Maya admitted. "I've always been focused on just doing the next thing . . . which, obviously, is not working well for me right now," she added flatly.

"Perhaps now would be a good time to start exploring this question," I suggested. "How you can recognize what *your* values are, as opposed to the achievements you feel like you're supposed to value, and how you can integrate those values into your life instead of the checklist? Would you be open to that?"

For Maya, this was the beginning of viewing her life through a new framework. Simply thinking about those two questions poked tiny holes in her beliefs about being good enough, eventually helping her appreciate that her hard work over the years had in fact rewarded her with a fulfilling life.

As Maya's story shows, we can absolutely find fulfillment in our achievements and even in the productivity habits that get us there. It is also extremely common to pursue achievements in a way that doesn't result in fulfillment. What differentiates these two experiences is how connected you are to your values.

In the book *Values in Therapy*, written by Jenna LeJeune and Jason Luoma, the authors discuss that being driven by personal values—things that are genuinely meaningful to you, as opposed to very specific goals and milestones—provides a direction for how to live your life.[5] One of the reasons toxic productivity is so depleting is that it leads us to ignore or deprioritize things that authentically matter to us. In contrast, productivity guided by values is sustainable precisely because it is not attached to milestones and timelines, but rather to our sense of purpose in life. When we do things that are aligned with our purpose, we experience deep fulfillment that naturally sustains our efforts. I know this probably sounds abstract, so let me explain using an example.

Let's say that you are a parent. Like all parents, you love your child and value their well-being—you want to be the "perfect" parent for them. However, you may have beliefs that cause you to doubt your own wisdom or ability as a parent and instead subscribe to society's expectations for parents. When you meet these expectations, you receive the reward of other people's validation—you feel like you belong, and that feels good! If you do not meet them, you reaffirm your own beliefs, feeling a sense of isolation, self-doubt, or even failure.

Therefore, if you parent through the lens of your need for belonging, you might base your decisions on what other parents are doing for their children or what milestones other children are achieving. Since your parenting decisions aren't based on your true values—in this case, fostering your child's individual well-being—you don't have an innate sense of direction for those decisions. Instead, your decisions are guided by comparing your child to other people's children, which is really a form of comparing yourself to other parents. While parenting this way might yield outward signs of success, it's also likely to make you and your child frustrated, overtired, and burned out.

The alternative is to base your parenting approach in your true value: your child's individual well-being. This would look like centering your child's interests and skills, as well as your connection with them, in the expectations you set and the decisions you make. While this approach may yield outcomes that are different from other children and parents, the quality of your life, your child's life, and your relationship with them, will improve. The inner reward you feel from parenting in alignment with your values gives you satisfaction, direction, and confidence in a way that chasing external milestones cannot.

Productivity driven by values means prioritizing what is truly important to you, rather than following the dictates of the external world. (Which, let's be honest, are always changing.) This allows you to step out of the toxic productivity mindset and learn how to be more engaged, more present, and more intentional with how you use your time and energy.

Values that Drive Healthy Productivity

You will have much more success in your productivity habits if you work toward goals that match the values that are important to you. Use the following questions to help identify two to three values that can guide you in life:

- Which aspects of life do you want to focus your energy on? (time, status, money, relationships, etc.)

- Are there any situations where you have said, "I can't do this; it's not who I am"? What were those situations? What did that tell you about yourself?

- What are some rules you live by?

Why Do We *Do* Instead of Just *Be*?

Have you ever been stuck in a traffic jam and the person behind you began to honk their horn, insisting you move even though there was nowhere for you to go? While this doesn't accomplish anything besides increasing frustration for everyone, there is actually a reason people behave this way—if not a good reason, at least a scientific reason. It's called the *action bias*.[6] In situations where we feel stuck, our brain favors doing *something*, even something unhelpful, because when a problem presents itself, doing nothing is too uncomfortable. Being still offers no distraction from a negative situation or the thoughts or feelings it brings up. In this example, honking the horn has the result of making the person feel better by taking action, releasing the building tension in a stressful moment.

At a healthy level, the action bias is a good thing. It moves you forward when you're in danger of getting stuck overthinking. For instance, if you just went on a date with someone and felt it went well, the action bias might motivate you to send a follow-up text message to see if they feel the same way. However, when action bias reaches an unhealthy level, it can be just as bad as the analysis paralysis we discussed in chapter 1, trapping you in a loop of action that has no result. Once you've sent the follow-up text message to your date, the action bias might turn unhealthy, pushing you keep checking your phone for their response or, worse, follow up on your follow-up text with even more messages. Even though you probably know deep down that this will hurt rather than help your chances of a second date, it feels in the moment like you're simply doing everything in your power to get what you want.

As we pursue acceptance and belonging, we seek to take action—a *lot* of action—and unhealthy action bias is a common indicator that our productivity habits have become toxic. But if more action isn't the answer, there must be a different route we can take. Let me explain this further with an example from one of my clients, Jeremy.

Jeremy, a 32-year-old man, started working with me to manage the anxiety he had about his romantic life. He struggled with comparing his relationship status to that of his friends, all of whom seemed to have found "the one" by then. His action bias led him to date multiple people at once, maintaining superficial connections, even with women he didn't feel very compatible with, rather than investing in just one relationship for a while. Being out on a date made him feel like he was *doing something* to change his relationship status.

"What do you value in a partner?" I asked.

"The usual, you know?" He seemed a little exasperated by my question. "I mean, what does anyone want? Getting along well, being interesting, physical attraction."

I tried to frame my question differently. "But when you think about a long-term partnership, what's important to you?"

"I think the most important thing about a partner is actually having one. My problem isn't that I can't find a certain 'type' of girlfriend. It's the fact that I can't find a girlfriend at all." He folded his arms, clearly frustrated that I couldn't understand him.

I gave our conversation a pause, letting him reflect on what he was saying. I did understand him. What I was trying to do was to get him to see a different perspective. For Jeremy, constantly setting up dates was less driven by a desire for emotional intimacy and connection, and more a handy distraction from the fear of being alone.

"Have you ever considered slowing down your dating 'schedule' or taking a break from dating altogether to think about what you want in a relationship?" I asked. "Doing that might help you figure out how you could meet a person who would be a good fit for you."

Unsurprisingly, the suggestion was met with resistance. "I've come here to therapy to figure out the issue and move *faster*," Jeremy said. "Slowing down will only keep me stuck where I am." He shifted around in his seat, fiddling with the buttons on his sweater.

"I know it feels that way," I started gently. "But surprisingly, slowing down is sometimes the fastest way to move forward. Right now, you're meeting a lot of people and hoping you'll find someone who 'clicks' with you. What if you were to take some time off dating to reflect on what you want in a partner and, more importantly, why you want one? Then you can concentrate your efforts on being more effective in dating instead of just having a high number of dates."

It is indeed a paradox how inaction can sometimes be the secret ingredient that makes you more productive. Rather than working on your goal until you can't think straight or until you collapse from tiredness, intentionally doing nothing for a while gives you the time and emotional energy to reflect on what you really need. This, in turn, empowers you to create a plan that aligns with those needs so that the actions you take will help you reach your goals.

For people stuck in the toxic productivity cycle, this paradox can be bewildering. Jeremy had a set of very strong beliefs about what a relationship meant and why he needed or deserved one. These deeply held beliefs fueled his conviction that slowing down the search for a partner was not an option. His perspective insisted that he didn't have time for thoughtful deliberation, let alone to consider that there might be other reasons for what was bothering him about being single. He shook his head at me, as if to say, "You just don't get it." The following week, he canceled our session, saying he would reschedule . . . but he never did. I could tell Jeremy was overwhelmed that I had disrupted his reasoning. It can be extremely difficult to challenge the things we tell ourselves, especially when those beliefs are foundational to who we have become.

Myths that Perpetuate Toxic Productivity

Every expression of toxic productivity is different because we all experience it for different emotional reasons, but I've found there are a few common foundational beliefs. Perhaps it would be more appropriate to call them *myths*—demonstrably false stories that we nevertheless believe without question because they are reinforced by familial, academic, professional, and cultural influences throughout our lives. These myths may be taught to us explicitly, but more often they are taught by example or packaged within aspirational concepts like "a strong work ethic" or "a drive for success."

As you read the following common toxic productivity myths, consider which ones resonate most with you:

- **Myth 1: Everything matters equally:** Dedicating the same amount of energy, attention, and time to every task means giving energy to things that might not require it. You might feel more productive filling up your calendar and to-do lists, but if those tasks and commitments don't move you closer to your goal or nourish you in the process, are you more productive? Or are you just staying busy?

  Vilfredo Pareto, an Italian economist and social scientist in the early twentieth century, found that often 80 percent of outcomes result from just 20 percent of the actions we take. Today, we refer to this as the Pareto Principle, though it's sometimes also known as "The Law of the Vital Few and the Trivial Many."[7] (I personally love this phrase because so much of what we think we must do can fall under "the trivial many.") If only 20 percent of our tasks actually impact about 80 percent of our lives, it stands to reason that we can't allocate the same importance to all the things we have to do.

  The reality: Some things are more important than others. Different tasks and behaviors have different priorities.

- **Myth 2: Multitasking helps us get more things done:** What we call multitasking is known among social scientists as *task-switching*.[8] When we think we are handling multiple tasks simultaneously, we're in fact shifting between different types of work, which means the brain is going back and forth among the tasks, using different parts to process multiple forms of information. This takes a heavy mental toll. It tires us out, both physically and mentally. The tiredness we feel persuades us that we are accomplishing more. However, what it really means is that we've done a lot without functioning as effectively. That's why multitasking so often looks like starting multiple things but not finishing them.[9] In fact, *monotasking*—starting and finishing one thing at a time—makes you more productive because you are able to complete the things you planned to with the ability of functioning at your highest level.

The reality: Multitasking is not actually possible for the human mind.

- **Myth 3: Working longer hours means getting more done:**[10] Research shows that the brain works in cycles of alertness every 90 minutes, much like our patterns of sleep. This alertness cycle is known as the body's *ultradian rhythm.*[11] Essentially, every 90 minutes or so, your body will start to signal fatigue through fidgetiness, hunger, and decreased focus. In order to achieve what you have set out to do, it's better to work with the body's natural rhythms instead of against them. This means taking intentional and regular breaks at that time your energy starts to dip so you can maintain your productivity over a sustained period of time.

  The reality: We are more productive when we work in short, concentrated bursts of effort instead of consistently working over long periods of time.

- **Myth 4: The only way to be more productive is to wake up early—ideally, earlier than everyone else:** The adage that "the early bird gets the worm" is not true for everyone. Research has shown that every person has a different circadian rhythm within their body, which means (among other things) that everyone has their own specific time when creative thinking and high-efficiency performance are at peak levels. For some, this peak does happen in the early morning, but for others, it comes in the late morning, afternoon, or evening. Instead of forcing yourself to be an early riser, you're better off developing a keen awareness of your body's rhythm and planning your day and activities to align with that rhythm as much as possible.

The reality: Pushing yourself to perform when you aren't at your productive best will only end up making (and keeping) you tired.[12]

Avoiding Autopilot

When working at the mental health start-up, I mentioned I was struggling with toxic productivity habits because of a lack of self-awareness. Another way of saying this is that I was running on *autopilot* mode, spending each day in a state of constant activity without intention or conscious connection to myself or the task. Just going through the motions. When you're in this mode, you wake up dreading the day ahead and end the day unable to recall what you did. Days blend into weeks, weeks blur into months, and you find yourself asking, *Where did all the time go?*

Occasional stress or overwhelm can cause any of us to go into autopilot mode from time to time. It's a survival strategy that disconnects you from your emotions. It is triggered by a sense of impending threat—essentially, the brain blocks out any thoughts or feelings related to the threat so that we can focus all our mental energy on avoiding the threat or solving the emergency. This threat can be anything: fear, confusion, anger, injustice, embarrassment. But living on autopilot is a serious problem. Similar to multitasking, this level of disconnection takes a heavy toll on our mental and emotional health. Let's take a look at how it affected my client, Sarah.

Sarah, a bright and motivated 25-year-old woman, started working with me because she was struggling to balance her career as a software developer with all the other responsibilities in her life. She also struggled with comparing her success to that of her friends, which fueled her desire for more productivity. This mindset led her to often working late into the evenings and over the weekends. Even though she knew that she shouldn't take on more projects at work, anytime her boss asked for volunteers to handle unassigned tasks, she invariably ended up raising her hand, hoping desperately that a promotion might be in her future. Unsurprisingly, this pattern left her no time and much less energy for self-care or a social life, but she felt like she needed to say yes to her friends so they would continue to invite her out.

"I know I should say no," she told me in one session, the self-judgment harshly present in her voice. "I can see my calendar is just jammed back-to-back with meetings. But I always convince myself that I'll work that evening, or I'll wake up early and work on a Saturday . . . I just overdo it."

"We all do things even when we know they are not good for us," I said. "Sometimes it's because we're thinking of the 'short-term pain/long-term gain' mindset. Sometimes it's because we're thinking *I've already committed so much, what's a little more?* Sometimes, we just don't know any better. I think what would be more helpful is to try to approach your habits from a place of curiosity. What do you think is going on behind the scenes for you?"

"I don't know. I think I just don't know what else to do," she said, teary-eyed. "Every time I have a free evening or a weekend, I feel compelled to fill up my time with . . . something. I feel like I should be making the most of my time. Even if I want to rest, I stress out trying to figure out the best way to do it. A lot of times, it ends up feeling easier to just get some more work done."

This is where autopilot brings us. We know we should do something differently, but our brain goes blank. For intelligent, high-achieving people like Sarah, this is particularly frustrating. It's important to understand that the mental "blank" isn't a failure of intelligence. It's simply what happens when old habits and chronic stress collide. The productivity-oriented routines that brought us to our current level of success have become a rut we can't get out of, and the pressure we experience (externally or self-imposed) inhibits the brain's ability to make even the simplest decisions, let alone think creatively or adapt to unfamiliar situations such as, say, a free weekend.

While increasing self-awareness is a vital first step, taking action on the knowledge your awareness yields requires breaking yourself out of autopilot mode. This starts with examining the beliefs, stories, and myths that drive your actions. Think of a habit of yours that you feel might be contributing to your toxic productivity, then ask yourself:

- *Where did I learn this habit or way of thinking?*

- *How does this stressful habit "reward" me?*

- *What do I think would happen if I stopped doing things this way?*

- *What would it mean for me to change this story about myself or even just to tweak it a little?*

To help Sarah find healthier ways to relate to productivity and herself, I invited her to reflect on some of her childhood experiences related to the problem she was feeling now. "What is your first memory of 'overdoing things'?" I asked.

After reflecting for a few minutes, Sarah admitted that overcommitting at school was historically her way of gaining her parents' acceptance. Even though it often led to episodes of deep exhaustion, and even a depressive episode in her late teens, this was the only way she knew to soothe the fear of rejection by her parents and the painful emotions of self-doubt, judgment, and shame that came with it.

Next, to help Sarah identify the beliefs that resulted from these formative experiences, we did something called *expressive writing*, a journaling exercise in which you set a timer and begin writing down your thoughts down exactly as they come to you, without censoring, changing, or editing. What makes this exercise unique, along with the stream of consciousness style, is that you are not allowed to stop writing until the timer goes off. This is powerful because it activates unfiltered expression, releasing thoughts you might not even be aware of and helping you gain insights into your behavior.

Exercise

Expressive Writing

1. Set a timer for three to five minutes and write down your answer to the following journal prompt. If you feel like you are stuck or don't have anything left to say, write out the thoughts that are coming to your mind about this exercise, a description of the room around you, a step-by-step prediction of what you will do for the rest of the day—whatever it takes to keep your hand moving. If new thoughts come to mind related to the journal prompt, switch back to that topic. Continue until the timer goes off.

   Prompt: What are your thoughts when you are resting?

   - What do you say about yourself? What is the quality and nature of your thoughts?

   - Whom does this voice belong to? Does it sound like one of your parents, a grade-school teacher, or another familiar figure?

   - How do you feel when you get these thoughts? What are the emotions (guilt, shame, stress, restlessness, etc.) you experience?

- ○ How would you categorize the quality of your thoughts? Are you being mean to yourself? Are you nurturing yourself?

2. Once your timer goes off, read through what you've written and highlight or underline any judgmental language that you notice. These might be labels, character judgments, or generalizations you're making about yourself.

3. Reflect on the parts you've highlighted. How many of those things are true? Which parts are false? Reflect on where you think you might have learned these judgmental words and the messages they imply.

4. Which of these statements can you reframe or rewrite to be more empowering?

Note: One way to reframe a negative or judgmental thought is to talk to yourself the way you would to a child or a friend. Another way is to talk about the behavior itself and not yourself.

I asked Sarah to continue doing this exercise at least once a day for 10 minutes, or anytime she had an opportunity to rest or even simply take a break from work. At our next session, we reviewed what she had written and, sure enough, I noticed a theme running through the thoughts she'd written down. The pattern that emerged from her pages was that saying no to opportunities at work triggered a belief for her: *If I say no, people will think I'm lazy, and I won't be valued anymore.* Overcommitting was her coping skill for dealing with her fear of rejection.

"What would a friend say to you if you said people will think you are lazy if you say no to something?" I asked.

"They'd probably say that saying no when I'm overworked actually makes me better at my job, and I bring a lot of value to the business already, so it won't be the end of the world."

"Do you believe that?"

Sarah burst out laughing because, of course, she didn't. Not yet, anyway. The beliefs she held about herself in relation to work were keeping her stuck in autopilot mode. Her fear of rejection and her coping skill for this fear were wired so deeply in her brain that even when she wanted to stop overcommitting, she simply couldn't think of what to do with her time instead. Recognizing this fear for what it was—an outgrowth of a false story about herself that she'd been taught in childhood—freed Sarah to apply her natural intelligence and creativity to rejecting her false beliefs, reframing them to be more accurate and uplifting, and ultimately developing a healthier relationship with productivity.

From Maya to Jeremy to Sarah, the stories in this chapter show how every expression of toxic productivity is different, as we all experience it for different emotional reasons based on past experiences, cultural myths, and messages we received as children. To break the cycle, you first need to understand the fears and feelings that your unhealthy habits help you avoid. Through regularly examining your beliefs about yourself and what your achievements say about you, you can begin to see the pattern of how your beliefs lead to your expression of toxic productivity. Identifying whether these beliefs truly belong to you or someone else from your life will help you decide whether they are accurate and, more importantly, supportive of your authentic values. If they are not, aim to reframe them into something more empowering and better aligned with what really matters to you.

Key Takeaways

- Productivity guided by values is more sustainable than goals based on milestones and timelines. When we work toward goals aligned with our values, we are more fulfilled by our efforts.

- People either use productivity habits to lean into a feeling of belonging through achievement or to avoid painful emotions such as shame, guilt, and rejection that arise because of the lack of belonging.

- Toxic productivity habits encourage us always to be in "doing" mode, even when that action is not actually helping us achieve a sense of belonging.

- Based on our background and environment, we might believe any of several myths about what it means to be productive. These myths often keep us trapped in the cycle of toxic productivity.

- Our routines can cause us to operate on autopilot, and the pressure to continue with what we know inhibits the brain's ability to think or adapt unfamiliar situations.

Chapter 3

The Many Masks of Toxic Productivity

"Beware the barrenness of a busy life."

—Attributed to Socrates

Thanks to the fear-based beliefs that give rise to toxic productivity, it embeds itself in our lives like a parasite, creating an agenda we carry in our minds no matter where we go or what we might be doing. Case in point: the year my partner and I decided to take a fully unplugged vacation. With our sights set on simply "being" instead of "doing," we took off for the island of Kauai with an intentional lack of organization. No itinerary, no plan for activities, no restaurant reservations—all we wanted to do was to hang out on the beach. But on the first day of the trip, as soon as our feet hit the sand, my mind went into agenda mode. I immediately started thinking about how to make the most of our beach day: considering whether this was our best window of time to be there, finding a place to sit that would get the most sun but also have proximity to shade, assessing the ideal distance from the waves and from other beachgoers.

Amid these mental gymnastics, I couldn't help noticing that my partner showed no concern about where we sat or who was close to us. As he napped next to me, his peaceful breaths keeping time with the waves breaking on the shore, I moved on to my next agenda item: write something interesting while sitting on the beach. At the time I believed that creative writers thrived in beautiful places; if I was going to be a good writer, it made sense for me to follow the same path. But to my frustration, no matter how hard I tried, I couldn't seem to write—certainly nothing as meaningful and profound as I expected to come from being in a place as magical as this small, secluded beach on Kauai's famous North Shore. I couldn't shake the feeling that I was wasting this opportunity to write. What's more, my partner and I had booked this trip to disconnect with work and connect with each other—I felt like I was wasting *that* opportunity as well.

Throughout the whole trip, I had many moments like this, where I struggled to be present and instead kept reverting to this subconscious agenda. Instead of rested and inspired, I felt both critical of my failure to produce some type of outcome and annoyed at myself for being so outcome-oriented, especially given that this was supposed to be a no-work trip. Clearly, my intention was different . . . but what *was* my intention, exactly?

After I got back home and reflected on the trip and all my feelings about it, I noticed a pattern: I'd been constantly looking for a way to maximize the value of the time we spent there, to make the most of every experience, every opportunity, every moment. There's nothing wrong with that, except that I was measuring that value by whether each experience produced a tangible outcome connected to a personal goal (such as being a better writer). Not only was this "making the most" mindset completely at odds with resting, the reason we'd booked the trip in the first place, but it hadn't even worked. Instead of helping me reach any personal goal, it made me feel annoyed, frustrated, and disappointed with myself.

Toxic productivity can show up under many different disguises. While our work life is an obvious breeding ground, the toxic mindset can also hide behind everyday actions like taking care of our home, spending time with our partner or children, or even self-care such as eating a healthy diet, working out, or (as in my story) taking a much-needed vacation. What differentiates truly healthy habits from toxic productivity is the intention we have behind them.

Productivity and Self-Care

"I think I just need to do more self-care," Maya said in a matter-of-fact tone. I looked up from my notes, caught off guard by her declaration. Weren't we just talking about how she could do *less*?

"You already do a lot of self-care," I reminded her. "How do you think adding more things to do will help you?" I watched her make calculations in her head.

After a few moments, she answered, "Aren't these the things that are supposed to help me grow as a person?" She paused, then continued. "The more healed I become by using these self-care practices, the easier it'll be for me to prioritize myself and say no to unnecessary projects at work."

To Maya, her self-care routine needed to look a specific way for her to believe that it was making an impact. It had to meet the markers she thought would "improve" her, including the things she saw on social media and what her friends were doing.

Maya is not alone in this mindset. Over the last decade or so, self-care has become a massive industry. It is everywhere: social media, magazines, TV shows, and even bus and subway ads. It seems like wherever you look, someone is telling you to do more for yourself. This saturation of self-care in our collective consciousness gives me pause, especially when I see a glossy ad promoting a new wellness product as the latest best thing in self-care. Consumerism-based wellness is fostering a harmful misunderstanding that makes self-care more akin to self-sabotage, like in Maya's case.

It's important to remember that self-care content is, in general, designed mainly to sell you something. Articles, videos, and blog posts can certainly be helpful for reminding you of the value of self-care or suggesting new rituals you might enjoy. But, at the risk of stating the obvious, true self-care begins with the *self*—that is, it's about what nourishes you as an individual. You are the best judge of what self-care looks like for you, not a magazine, celebrity, or motivational speaker with a product or a program to sell. Moreover, self-care is flexible—what works for you will change as your needs, preferences, or circumstances change.

When you are struggling with toxic productivity, it becomes difficult to see self-care as an end in itself. Instead, it becomes easy to see self-care as a means to an end. Maya was justifiably looking for fulfillment from things other than work or life "milestones." Her instinct that focusing on her own needs would achieve this was a good one. But because of how deeply toxic productivity was embedded in her mindset, her efforts at self-care had the same effect on her as overworking. In the name of relaxation and recharging, she filled her Sunday mornings with rituals and activities culled from social media videos that were more aspirational than inspirational.

"What if we simplified your self-care?" I proposed. "What if you didn't do *anything*?" At Maya's blank stare, I offered a little more detail. "What would it feel like if next Sunday, instead of going to the gym, then to the farmers' market to buy yourself flowers, then home to make a green smoothie, you just slept in as self-care?"

Maya didn't hesitate. "I would feel like I wasted my Sunday morning," she said.

"Why is it a waste to sleep and rest your body?" I countered.

"Because it's lazy, and I don't want to be a lazy person."

Bingo. There it was: her intention for self-care was not to care for herself, but to use it to feel good about herself. The items on her self-care list weren't inherently bad or harmful, but what is harmful is the pressure she put on herself to do them. Without realizing it, Maya had simply swapped out the environment in which she was practicing toxic habits. Instead of practicing self-care with the goal of feeling good, she was practicing it in order to feel good enough.

Truthfully, Maya's situation reminded me a little of my own struggle. I know how difficult everything seems, even simply caring for yourself, when it's attached to the goal of achieving an idealized version of yourself. Under this kind of pressure, there is almost no winning—only shame and guilt if you don't do it, and disappointment and criticism if you don't do it well enough. (And let's be honest: when does an overachiever ever think they've done something well enough?)

Exercise

Are Your Self-Care Habits Turning Toxic?

Let's take a few minutes to reflect on your self-care habits. The following list includes some of the signs that you might be using self-care as a disguise for toxic productivity:

- Your rules about what self-care should look like are very rigid and restrictive.

- When you don't engage in self-care practices, you feel ashamed or like a failure.

- The goal of your self-care practice is working toward an imagined ideal self, so you have set high standards and expectations for yourself.

  If any of these apply to you, become curious about what is motivating your self-care habits. Consider the following questions, and journal your response if you'd like:

  - What type of self-care activities make you feel better? How often do you do these things?

  - What are you hoping that self-care gives you?

  - How do you feel when you skip self-care? What thoughts come up if you don't do the self-care activity you had in mind?

If you suspect your self-care habits are a mask for toxic productivity, you can find a way out by becoming attuned to your emotional needs. With that in mind, I nudged Maya to reflect on her feelings before and after her current self-care practice. For example, how did she feel most Sunday mornings when her alarm went off? Was the farmers' market really enjoyable for her, especially after rushing there from gym to catch the last few minutes before it closed? What about Sunday nights? After a full day of "self-care" activities, did she feel a sense of confidence or dread when she looked ahead to the tasks and obligations of her workweek?

These questions helped Maya realize that forcing herself to do self-care based on "should" was not meeting her needs of resting—that it was, in fact, the opposite of resting. It was only adding to the exhaustion and overwhelm she was battling at work.

To get thinking about how she could replace the laundry list of self-care "shoulds" with things that offered genuine rest and nourishment, we listed out every activity in the routine she typically followed on Sundays. Next to each activity, we wrote down the "should" behind it—what was each of these activities supposed to accomplish for her? If it was a negative "should," like her goal of getting up early to avoid being a lazy person, we crossed it off the list. If it was a positive "should," such as helping her be playful or experience peace or joy, we considered whether the activity was actually hitting the "relax and recharge" mark for her. Did buying flowers at the farmers' market truly feel like giving herself a treat? Did she even like those green smoothies she was making? When the activity didn't hit the mark, we explored things she used to do as a child that gave her that feeling she was seeking. When the activity was hitting the mark, we considered how she could get the same effect from a smaller dose of the activity. For instance, if she did decide to sleep in, maybe taking a long walk to the botanical gardens could be as good as an early morning at the gym and a rushed visit to the farmers' market.

These questions helped Maya reconnect with herself physically, mentally, and emotionally. Nourishing this connection is what self-care is really all about. Instead of treating your own needs like just another box to check, try responding to them with the care and attention you'd crave from a loving parent or an attentive partner. Not only will this help you get off the hamster wheel of industrialized self-care so you can save your resources for what really nourishes you, but it can also be the beginning of reclaiming your mindset in all areas of your life. (We will explore self-care in more depth in chapter 10.)

Productivity and Personal Development

One of the most harmful masks that toxic productivity can wear is the mask of personal development. There's nothing wrong with the desire to learn how to be a better version of ourselves or to improve our performance in ways that matter to us. But when self-improvement efforts meet toxic productivity's emphasis on making us feel "good enough," it typically results in goals that are overly broad or vague. Rather than working on how we can be a better friend, partner, or steward of our own time and talents, we're simply trying to become "better." Without a specific purpose or application, personal development becomes a joyless exercise, never yielding any rewards or fulfillment from our efforts.

Even where there is a specific purpose to your personal development, a toxic mindset will undermine your efforts. Toxic productivity thrives on absolutes. Our efforts are either successes (perfectly achieved) or else they are failures. In the face of this pressure to perform our hobbies and personal interests "perfectly," we often simply let them go. For another thing, the toxic mindset makes success a moving target. As soon as you hit your stride in one area of your life, you'll find another area that needs improving before you can feel good enough. In short, a toxic mindset changes personal development from being a helpful means of achieving your goals to a goal in itself. This is what my client Julia had been struggling with.

Julia, a woman in her thirties, started therapy after recognizing that she wasn't living a life that she felt happy with. This feeling permeated different areas of her life: work, romantic relationships, how she felt about herself, and her relationship with her mother.

Along with a number of personal and professional goals she wanted to meet (finding and keeping a healthy relationship, building a career that contributed to the world and aligned with her values), she wanted to dedicate time and effort to being a better person. Many of our conversations were about the next course or bootcamp she could sign up for, a spiritual retreat she could attend, or other ways to improve her life skills, personally and professionally.

After a few of these conversations, certain patterns began to emerge. I noticed that her personal development goals were often framed by negative assessments about herself: "If only I had graduated from a better university," "I wasted so much time before," "I don't know how to make good decisions," "I'm such a mess," "My college friends are all making so much more money than me." I also noticed that she often jumped from one thing to another, starting but seldom finishing. While she'd be initially consumed by the idea of what a new skill or opportunity could offer her, she struggled to follow through, citing some other area of her life that was holding her back. These patterns showed me that her intention for pursuing personal development was less about pursuing happiness and more about outrunning her own sense of inferiority.

Exercise

Are Your Personal Development Habits Turning Toxic?

Let's take a few minutes to reflect on your personal development habits. The following list includes some of the signs that you might be using personal development as a disguise for toxic productivity:

- You continuously buy self-help and personal development books even though you already own many and haven't read them yet. Your unread pile of books makes you feel guilty for not focusing on yourself.

- You feel pressured to take more courses, attend conferences, or join more peer groups to feel like you're as smart or knowledgeable as your peers. You have a fear of missing out on opportunities.

- You consume social media content (podcasts, TikTok and Instagram videos, articles, etc.) exclusively from self-help teachers and influencers. You often feel bad about yourself after watching the videos.

- If you are in therapy, you strive to be the "best" therapy client rather than an authentic one, and you resist sharing your true self with your therapist.

- You have a vague goal of getting better at one or multiple areas of your life, but you don't have a concrete focus. You might even jump from one goal to another every few months.

If any of these apply to you, become curious about what is motivating your personal development efforts. Consider the following questions, and journal your response if you'd like:

- When you pursue personal development, do you feel better?

- Does pursuing achievement or productivity make you feel like you have more control in your life? What are you trying to control?

- How do you feel when you are not pursuing personal development?

Identifying your intention for personal development will give insight into whether you are approaching it from a healthy mindset or a toxic productivity mindset. If the intention is coming from a toxic mindset ("I am not good enough if I don't have _____ skill"), you'll stay stuck in your own sense of deficiency no matter how much effort you put forth. More likely, though, you'll never find the motivation to follow through on what you start, because a toxic mindset will always undermine your efforts with some new way that you're falling short. If the intention is coming from a healthy mindset ("Having _____ skill will make it easier for me to show up the way I want to in ____ area of my life"), any efforts you make will be successful; in this case, successful means that this change will either help you grow or, at the very least, refine your thinking about how you want to grow. A healthy mindset also makes it easier to build momentum on our self-improvement journey—we stay out of our own way by acknowledging our shortcomings without judgment and increase strength by appreciating ourselves for the small successes we experience from one day to the next.

In short, a healthy approach to personal development involves practicing *self-acceptance*. To help counter Julia's tendency to hop from one self-improvement effort to another, we began starting our sessions with a recap of one thing she was proud of herself for doing over the last week. We took a moment for Julia to appreciate her win, congratulate herself for the effort she'd put in, reflect on the natural strengths and resilience that had supported her effort, and connect it to previous successes so that she could savor how much progress she'd already made. We also worked on rephrasing any judgmental language she used about herself in sessions. When Julia began to focus on how certain habits, traits, or past experiences were holding her back, I prompted her to instead acknowledge those things in an empathetic and supportive way, the way she would talk to a dear friend or a child. This helped her start to see herself as a whole person, with space for both acceptance and growth.

Self-acceptance involves cultivating a holistic view of yourself, giving as much attention to what you already do well and how far you've come as to what you can do better or why you're falling short. Self-acceptance helps you see yourself as a dynamic and changing individual, which allows you to be flexible with your efforts at self-improvement rather than seeing them as complete failures if you don't see success right away. Self-acceptance reframes personal development as a lifelong journey rather than a "once and for all" goal.

Productivity and Chronic Busyness

I sometimes refer to my work as a therapist as window cleaning, wiping away the "smudges" of denial, rationalization, and repression from my clients' field of vision so they can see their lives more clearly. Never was this role more clear than with my client, Lara.

Lara was a sharp, intelligent lawyer and mother of two. Without looking at her phone calendar, she could list out all the things she had scheduled and planned, and describe in detail the benefit each thing would bring to her family.

As a therapist who predominantly works with millennial urban professionals, most of my clients struggle with being chronically busy. Lara came to work with me because she was struggling in her marriage. Actually, it would be more accurate to say that her husband, Sam, was struggling because he felt their family's lives were too busy at Lara's behest. The issue Lara wanted to work on in therapy was his perception. She wanted to change her husband's view on busyness, to help him instead see her as ambitious and motivated to make a great life for their family.

Now, usually I don't like to frame my client's presenting issue through the lens of another person. But, within twenty minutes of our first session, I realized Sam's perception was accurate.

"You mentioned last week that Sam says you're too busy," I started. "What do you think makes him say this?"

"He complains that I don't spend any 'downtime' with him," Lara answered. "But there's just a lot to be done. Our children see an after-school tutor and then go to piano lessons, which means I have to leave work early to shuttle them everywhere. And I want to be present with them in the evenings, so that usually means I'm finishing up work after they're in bed."

"What about Saturdays?" I asked.

"The kids play tennis on Saturdays," she answered.

"Sundays?"

"The kids don't have anything scheduled on Sundays," she acknowledged, "but I'm usually up early and out the door for a volunteer committee at my workplace." She added, "I studied and worked for 15 years to get to where I'm at professionally—of course I'm going to make the most of my opportunities. What, I'm supposed to throw it all away just to sit around the house on a Sunday?"

Lara's breathless defense of her schedule left me a bit out of breath too. I paused to let her words settle, then continued.

"And how satisfied are you with the amount of time you spend with your family?"

"I mean, we spend *all* our time together. Anytime we're not at work, we're with each other and the kids." She halted, reflecting. "Yeah, sure, I get a little irritated at times and I'm usually too tired at night for . . . you know . . . with my husband. But, I mean, my days are long and when I get to bed, I just want to sleep." She looked down. "I do feel guilty about it, and I'm always trying to make it up to him. I figure if I can get a little more ahead at work, then we'll have extra time to spend together." She met my eyes with a look that said what we both understood: the "extra time" never materialized.

Lara couldn't see what laid behind everything she was doing: the never-ending quest to feel like the perfect mother, perfect spouse, perfect coworker, perfect *everything*. I didn't want to ask Lara to consider if all this busyness really counted as being there for her husband or kids—that would only invite more defensiveness. What I wanted her to think about was how well she was being there for herself. Was it all truly fulfilling to her? What was she afraid might happen if she stopped being busy?

47

"What's rewarding for you about having such a packed schedule?" I asked. "You said you feel a little irritated and guilty sometimes— what makes it worth it to keep going, even when you feel that way?"

"Being able to do all the things I do makes me feel responsible. I'm a person who is driven to succeed and I don't think there's anything wrong with that. I want to show my kids that being successful takes hard work and dedication. As for the sacrifices, they seem worth it because it will give my kids the best possible start in life."

"But what makes them worthwhile for *you*?" I continued to nudge. "Would it be fair to say that a packed schedule makes you feel competent and valued by others around you? Like you are needed?"

This question shifted something inside Lara; I could see it in the way her face changed. It seemed to have brought her into confrontation with thoughts or feelings that she had been avoiding. Wiping away tears that had started to form in the corner of her eyes, she nodded without speaking.

There is nothing inherently wrong with wanting to make the most of our time and talents, to do right by the people who count on us, to set a good example. What we must consider is who really benefits from our busyness. In Lara's case, her commitment to her kids' extracurricular activities seemed to not be entirely about their education; it had a lot to do with her needing to feel like a responsible, successful mother. We must also consider whether the benefit is worth the cost to us. Is the glow of feeling needed worth the exhaustion that builds, week after week, as we scurry from one commitment to the next?

Chronic busyness sustains toxic productivity by focusing on quantity over quality regarding the things you do. For a while, we might regard them as the same—the adrenaline high of getting more done (quantity) makes us feel like we're on top of the world (quality).

For some, that high ends with a crash, leaving them exhausted and burned out. For others, like Lara, the high gradually levels off, offering less fulfillment to their underlying emotional needs. Rather than examine those emotional needs, they find a new commitment to elicit the feeling they crave.

As with the earlier story about toxic productivity masquerading as self-care, the "cure" for this situation is becoming attuned to your emotional needs. But for people like Lara—hooked on the high of productivity—identifying the real need under the busyness can feel particularly vulnerable. Those who have spent a lifetime compensating for this emotional need through productivity and overachievement might not even be able to pinpoint what the emotion is.

"Lara, we've been talking about how there is a disconnect between how you view your schedule and how your husband views it," I said. "I wonder if there's a way you can reflect on your schedule from a new perspective—focusing less on the tasks you do, and more on how you feel about them. Sometimes our feelings are like messengers. They are giving us information, and if we can learn to hear that message, it will help us recognize what needs to change."

Lara considered in silence. "Okay. But we don't always feel good about what we do, even when it's good for us. So how will we know whether it's a message we should listen to or not?"

That's a great question, I thought.

"This is true. Some emotions are reactions to how we're feeling about a task in the moment. However, if we pay attention to our emotions over the course of days or weeks, we can be more confident that they are sending a message we should listen to. For example, if you notice that you tend to feel angry, antagonistic, or bitter toward a person or your schedule without a specific incident or reason, that's a sign that things are off balance. Disproportional reactivity or irritability is another—when small annoyances start to consistently feel out of proportion, it is an indication that your emotional resources are depleted. This is known as *emotional literacy*, and it works like a muscle—the more we use it, the stronger it becomes."

Are Your Busyness Habits Turning Toxic?

Let's take a few minutes to reflect on your busyness habits. The following list includes some of the signs that you might be using busyness as a disguise for toxic productivity:

- You're seen as competent, even if it's driven by underlying anxiety.

- You have unrealistic expectations of yourself and others. You live by the ethos of always aiming high, shooting for the stars, or thinking big.

- Your friends and family often call you an overachiever. You find it difficult to slow down even when you're burned out.

- You say yes first, then think about how you can accommodate the request.

- You commit to too many things and feel like you're always short on time.

If any of these apply to you, become curious about what is motivating your chronic busyness. Consider the following questions, and journal your response if you'd like:

- What are the advantages and disadvantages in your life of maintaining a consistently busy schedule?

- Are there any areas in your life that are being neglected or compromised due to your busyness?

- *And the question I asked Lara*: How would you feel if your schedule was less packed? What fears, if any, come up for you when considering this possibility?

Because so many of our toxic productivity habits are a way of coping with uncomfortable emotions, building emotional literacy is an important part of healing. If we can learn to recognize our emotions, hear their message, and address them in a healthy way, we're well on our way to breaking out of the toxic mindset.

Productivity Habits and Emotional Needs

You know by now that toxic productivity behaviors are commonplace in those yearning for a sense of validation, acceptance, and belonging from others. Another way of saying it is that toxic productivity is a way of getting our emotional needs met. According to psychologist Abraham Maslow's hierarchy of needs and the work of cognitive psychologist Scott Barry Kaufman, our core emotional needs include:[13, 14]

- **Safety:** The need for secure relationships and emotional and physical environments
- **Connection:** The need to be accepted by others
- **Self-esteem:** The need to have a positive sense of self
- **Exploration:** The need for growth through new experiences
- **Love:** The need for emotional intimacy
- **Purpose:** The need for a central meaning to what you do

Some of us learn early on that we only feel a sense of belonging within our families (safety) or receive affection (love), attention (connection), or praise (self-esteem) when we meet our caregivers' expectations for obedience, conformity, or achievement. Messages like "You are mommy's favorite little boy—you got such great grades on your exam" and "Look at that little girl—look how she behaves—what are they going to think of us when they see you acting like this?" litter the childhoods of almost everyone I know.

Now, as an adult, you believe that love, connection, and maybe even safety require some sort of behavioral "barter" from you; you must work hard, succeed, and be enough, and these achievements must be recognized by others, particularly those in authority over you or those you admire. It's only natural, then, that you believe relentless productivity is the answer to getting your emotional needs met in relationships—familial, platonic, or romantic. However, this feeling of emotional fulfillment is temporary, only lasting as long as the glow of your latest achievement. It's also illusory; human beings don't form those types of emotional bonds based on seeing someone's résumé. Despite what your brain has learned since childhood, people don't feel more connected to you because of your achievements, and the validation or sense of belonging you feel when you excel is not the same as real love, connection, or safety.

Admittedly, the world we live in doesn't make it easy to break this illusion. Our culture equates being busy with being productive, and being productive means being in the good graces of others. There's nothing quite like the rush of presenting your boss with a list of tasks you've accomplished before they even thought to ask, or seeing your calendar packed full of social events with people who want to spend time with you. It feels like tangible proof that you are a capable, interesting, desired person. Even when the charm of constant busyness turns to exhaustion, the idea of fewer commitments might trigger fears of losing the professional and social capital you've gained—in other words, not being as "wanted" as you were before.

This was certainly the case with Maya. When I asked her why she needed to work so much, late into the nights and on weekends, sometimes even skipping social events like birthdays and brunches, she told me it was to further her career so she could meet her milestones. But when I began asking about how she grew up, I learned that her family's social circle was made up of high-earning, ultra-successful professionals. As a result, she felt pressure to climb the corporate ladder to feel a greater sense of belonging with her community.

"What about the idea of working less feels hard for you?" I asked.

"I don't want to be left out," she mumbled. "If everyone goes on a trip or to a party, I want to be able to go and not hang back just because I can't afford it." She shifted uncomfortably in her chair and kept her eyes on the floor.

"Is sharing this with me bringing up any feelings?"

"Yeah, I . . ." She continued to study the carpet. "It feels stupid. Like my friends are only my friends because I can afford to be friends with them. I know that's not true, but . . ."

The fact was that Maya didn't know this wasn't true. Her emotional foundation told her that to feel connected with her social circle, she had to fit in. Like Lara, Maya saw the sacrifice of overworking as worthwhile because she believed it would eventually make her feel more connected to her friends. Meanwhile, though, she was missing out on actual opportunities to connect with them in real life.

Are You Using Productivity to Meet Your Emotional Needs?

Let's take a few minutes to reflect on how you get your emotional needs met. The following list includes some of the signs that you are using toxic productivity to meet your emotional needs:

- You struggle with setting boundaries and saying no to additional commitments. You take on more than you can handle and often overextend yourself.

- Even though you accomplish your tasks, you feel unsatisfied and unfulfilled.

- You have anxious thoughts about failure and can't fight the feelings that you are falling behind or not meeting expectations.

- You feel that people around you will show you respect or affection if you say yes to their requests.

If any of these apply to you, become curious about how you view your emotional needs. Consider the following questions, and journal your response if you'd like:

- Think back to a time where you felt fulfilled emotionally. What activities, experiences, people, or moments made you feel this way?

- Which of the six main core emotional needs (safety, connection, self-esteem, exploration, love, purpose) are most important to you?

- How do you prioritize your emotional needs in daily life? What areas require more attention or balance?

The alternative to meeting your emotional needs through toxic productivity habits is to prioritize emotionally safe and healthy relationships. You can do this by identifying what your boundaries are for emotional connection. This will help you find relationships that meet your core emotional needs in a healthy way. Reflect on the times when you feel anxiety or pressure to conform in relationships and notice if there are any patterns that make you feel this way. Think about what can change in these relationships for you to feel emotionally satisfied or safer. The more meaningful your emotional connections are, the less you will turn to toxic productivity (or other unhealthy dynamics) to meet your emotional needs.

The Sandcastle Lesson

As a therapist, I've learned that many of the daily struggles we have in our lives are connected to a deeper issue—one that we ourselves might not even see clearly at the time. During that discouraging afternoon on the beach in Kauai, I would have told you I was struggling with being creative. But when I reflected on it later, I realized I was really struggling with a low sense of self-worth. While I hadn't brought my laptop on the trip, I had brought along a very specific standard of what it meant to be a "good enough" writer. My toxic productivity mindset had turned our vacation into a work trip for me.

I was broken out of my rumination by the sound of my partner's voice. He was down by the water, and the breaking waves swallowed most of his words. All I could hear was "... sandcastles...!"

"Sandcastles?" I called back, confused.

He cupped his hands around his mouth. "Do you know how to make sandcastles?"

Dropping to the ground, he started to dig a hole. With my writing efforts going nowhere, I went down to join him, and after a few moments of effort, I realized the answer to his question was no. At 34 years old, with two degrees and a packed résumé to my credit, I had no idea how to make a sandcastle. I'd never done it before!

In an effort to help, I poured water into the hole he was digging. Immediately, the moat around the castle foundation began to flood. Laughing, we started again. Even though my water had washed away all the work he had done, just sitting and laughing about it made the whole thing feel more like vacation than anything my perfect planning had accomplished that day.

As the sun moved slowly westward across the sky and the high tide began to find its way back home, my productivity-obsessed thoughts receded into the backdrop. I was flooded with the abundance that surrounded us: gulls swooping down to meet the sea, the sounds of children playing, the warm grit of sand under my hands. When we finally sat back to admire our lumpy, crumbling castle, I noticed that the sun was nothing but a thin pink line on the horizon. We'd been there for hours, just working on our sandcastles; I couldn't remember the last time I'd been this immersed in a single project, so deeply connected with what I was working on that I had not worried about anything except what was in front of me. Looking up at my partner, who was still proudly smiling at our handiwork, I realized it had been a long time since I'd felt this connected to him, too.

Key Takeaways

- Toxic productivity can disguise itself as personal development and self-care habits, which makes it difficult to identify because they are socially acceptable and seen as beneficial.

- Performing habits with toxic intentions will leave you stuck in your own deficiency, undermining your efforts no matter what; doing so with healthy intentions will help you grow, no matter how successful you are.

- Toxic productivity can show up as being chronically busy and can lead to overextending yourself.

- Toxic productivity can be motivated by a desire to meet unmet emotional needs and feel connected to others, leading you to erroneously believe that the more you accomplish, the more connection you will feel.

Chapter 4

Using Productivity as Self-Worth

"Be gentle with yourself. You are a child of the universe no less than the trees and the stars; you have a right to be here."

—Max Ehrmann, *Desiderata*

By now, it's probably becoming clear to you that many of our toxic productivity habits are, at their core, less about the thing we want to achieve and more about how that achievement relates to our inner sense of self. Toxic productivity can help us seem worthy in other people's eyes, but much more importantly, it promises to *us* an increase in self-respect, a greater self-confidence, an improvement in expressing self-love, and of course, a strong sense of self-esteem and self-worth.

While both self-worth and self-esteem are connected to your sense of success and well-being, understanding the difference between them is important when it comes to overcoming toxic productivity.[15] *Self-esteem* is your evaluation of your external self-image based on your skills, accomplishments, capabilities and other people's perception of you.[16, 17] *Self-worth*, on the other hand, refers to your subjective conceptualization of your own worthiness. It is an internal map of how you see yourself—specifically, if you feel "good enough" to belong among the people you admire or feel an affinity with.[18, 19] In short, self-esteem is about what you think you should deserve, while self-worth is about what you feel you do deserve.

Toxic Productivity and Self-Worth

Low self-worth can show up in subtle ways, especially as negative thoughts or interpretations of others' reactions. These can fuel the toxic productivity mindset, constantly egging you on to do more so that you will feel more worthy. The following list includes some examples of emotional dynamics that might come up when you struggle with low self-worth:

- **Self-doubt:** You constantly doubt yourself and the quality of your output, or what you bring to the table. You might think to yourself, *"Am I good enough?"*

- **People-pleasing:** You measure yourself and your achievements and productivity using the yardstick of other people's validation. You might think to yourself, *"Are they happy with me?"*

- **Indecisiveness:** You question your judgment and skills. You might think to yourself, *"I can't make the right decisions."*

- **Productivity dysmorphia:** You feel guilty about not achieving the goals you set for yourself in relationships and at work, even when you're accomplishing a reasonable number of tasks. You might think to yourself, *"I have not done enough."*

- **Impostor syndrome:** You question the place you take in other people's lives and whether you belong there. You might think to yourself, *"They'll find out I'm not really good at this/for them."*

- **Perfectionism:** You think everything you do needs to be of a high standard, and you have a hard time giving yourself grace for failures and mistakes. You might think to yourself, *"I can't make any mistakes."*

- **Self-betrayal:** You dismiss, ignore, or avoid your emotional needs for the sake of meeting your goals. You might think to yourself, *"It doesn't matter what I want, what matters is what I should do."*

In chapter 2, I shared my story of working at a rapidly growing start-up while also trying to grow my own wellness platform on the side. Unsurprisingly, the punishing schedule resulted in intense burnout that eventually led me to quit my job. The interesting thing was that even though I had mulled over the decision for months, finally making the move didn't immediately bring the relief I expected. Instead, within the first two weeks of quitting, I started to feel like because I wasn't working, I didn't "exist" in the world; it was as if my "worth" to society had suddenly plummeted with a single decision. Nothing else about my life had changed; I had the same friends, the same loving partner and family, the same home. But with no work to do, no productivity to show, I felt a quiet whisper in the back of my mind: *Who are you now?*

I began to worry about how I would introduce myself to new people. After all, "What do you do?" is one of the most common questions to ask when we meet new people. It's a way of showing interest in someone, a gateway into learning more about them. However, the question carries a subtle implication that perhaps the most distinctive or defining aspect of your life is what you do. This might not always be true everywhere, but in a career-driven city like New York, the question is more often than not used to determine how relatable you are to someone else or, worse, to make assumptions about your lifestyle and social status. I could only imagine the thoughts in others' minds as I told them, "I'm working on a new opportunity," or even worse, "I'm not doing anything right now."

Driven by this worry, I laid out a detailed plan for my "(f) unemployment" time: wake up at 7 a.m. to meditate and work out, have a green smoothie and write in my journal before turning on my laptop at 9 a.m., then get to work on an article for publication or creating mental health education content for my newly launched digital wellness platform, which I'd, of course, have finished by the end of the day. Some days, I woke up feeling motivated enough to take on the world and would dive into my entrepreneurial tasks without missing a beat. Other days, though, I would wake up feeling overwhelmed, both by the volume of work I expected myself to complete and by the stretch of empty time ahead of me if I didn't.

Reflecting on that time now, I have to laugh at myself. Here I was with a rare window of time in which I had no one to report to, no external workload to complete, no schedule to abide by—why, instead of enjoying that time, was I stressing more than ever over being productive?

The answer is that productivity made me feel purposeful. Working hard, and the achievements that came with it, gave me an enormous portion of my self-worth. Especially during that transition period of my life, being productive made me feel like I was still on par with my friends and peers who were working and furthering their careers.

What Makes Productivity So Important?

Take a moment to think about the title of this exercise. Why do *you* find productivity so important? Use the following questions as a way to begin examining your thoughts on your own self-worth:

- What are the words you would use to describe yourself?
- What does *worth* mean to you? What parts of you are worth the most?
- What values do you think you bring to others in your life?
- What external aspects of your life have the greatest connection with your sense of value? Is it your personal attributes (styles, skills, etc.), your job title and salary, where you live, your relationships status, or something else?

The answers to this exercise will help you begin to reflect on how you view your worthiness outside of productivity.

Your Core Beliefs and You

"So much of me rejects me."

Julia said this while we were working together to figure out why she felt empty no matter how often she traveled, how many romantic relationships she had, or how interesting her jobs had been over her career. Our conversation revealed her deep ambivalence about herself. She genuinely felt there was a split between how others viewed her and how she viewed herself. These feelings spoke to a deep-rooted core belief: *On my own, I am not enough for others to love me and for me to belong.*

Remember from chapter 1 that our core beliefs serve as the blueprint for how we navigate relationships, approach work, and treat ourselves. We develop core beliefs throughout our childhood and early adulthood, through experiences with our caregivers, siblings, friends, romantic partners, and peers.

Our core beliefs are instilled through emotion rather than through reason. When we're taught something as children by the people who care for us—whether a healthy message or something more toxic—we instinctively adhere to it out of loyalty and love toward those people. Likewise, when we are part of an unexpected experience, especially a challenging one, we unconsciously draw a lesson from it to guide our choices in the future. The belief formation is primal, a survival reaction; to reinforce it, the mind looks for evidence to support the core belief and filters out any evidence against it. We begin building a story around this belief that contains our thoughts about other people in our lives—why they treat us the way they do and how we must behave with them to get what we want and need.

The instinct to trust our core beliefs is so deeply embedded in the human brain that we might not notice when it's happening, even when the "evidence" that supports these beliefs is wildly illogical or manifestly false. This is why it's important to fact-check the assumptions you have about yourself and the conclusions you draw when something happens to you. Let's say you have a core belief that says, *I am not good at anything.* If you, for example, get a promotion at work, your brain will do anything to support this core belief, creating automatic thoughts like *I just got lucky—they probably made a mistake,* or *They just needed someone to fill the role.* In doing this, your thoughts work hard to negate your success and its positive implication about you.

Why does the brain do this to us? Why does it find reasons to keep us in a state of low self-worth, even when there is plenty of evidence to the contrary? It's because the brain tends to hold onto negative thoughts and memories more strongly than positive ones. This is known as *negativity bias,* and while it may sound counterproductive, it has an evolutionary purpose.[20] This is how the brain evolved to ensure that you don't repeat the same mistakes or miss signs of a dangerous situation you've experienced before.

The problem is that when the negative thoughts and memories are bound up with a subconscious core belief about yourself, it makes the negativity a lot harder to unearth, and even more difficult to change. The brain is determined to keep you safe from emotional danger as well as physical danger. A childhood in which your bids for love and connection were repeatedly met with rejection (parents' disappointment at low grades, lack of conformity, other performance-related transgressions, etc.) will persuade the brain that it is dangerous to believe you inherently deserve love and connection. Therefore, it nips any self-worth in the bud so you'll never run the risk of rejection again; it instead pushes you toward the core belief that achievement, conformity, and perfect performance will earn the love and connection you desire. This is how a person can end up with high self-esteem but unwittingly struggle with low self-worth.

One day, almost three months after he had stopped coming to sessions, I got an email from Jeremy: *Hi Israa, I know we haven't talked in some time. A woman I'd been dating for the last two months just broke up with me, and I feel like I don't even know where to begin. I'm tired of feeling so bad about myself. Can we meet again?*

From our previous work together, I'd noted that Jeremy had a very strong cause-effect belief about relationships and success. In his own words, he was "in a place in his life where he should be in a committed relationship." When he compared himself to his already partnered friends, he saw himself as having all the necessary "qualifications" to be in a relationship. But his frustration and impatience with dating revealed a core belief that he was not good enough on his own— he needed to be in a romantic relationship in order to feel good about himself. In short, he had high self-esteem but low self-worth. I emailed Jeremy back, agreeing to resume our work together. Once we were in session, though, I encouraged him that should he disagree with me or feel like something wasn't right, it would be better for him to share that with me instead of abruptly stopping coming to sessions.

"Ghosting your therapist can be harmful for you," I said. "It holds you back from learning how to confront people you might disagree with in a healthy way. I don't take it personally at all if you disagree with me. You need to know that you have this space to say whatever you need."

"So, I don't have to agree with you all the time?" he asked.

I hid a smile. "No, you don't have to agree with me all the time. All I ask is that you consider what I'm saying in response to what you share with me and respond honestly about it rather than disappearing. Okay?" I shifted the session to our therapeutic work. "So, tell me what happened with this woman you were seeing."

Jeremy crossed his arms. "She said I was trying to move too fast, but I didn't think so. I just wanted to get serious."

"It sounds like you were not on the same page as her. Is 'getting serious' something you talked about together?"

"No, not really," he admitted. "I mean, women say they want a deeper connection, commitment. But then when I tried to go there, she said I was 'rushing it.'" He rolled his eyes.

"Do you think you were rushing it?" I asked.

"Of course! But why is that a bad thing? I'm ready for the next stage in my life. I want to be in a serious relationship, and I really wanted to move forward on that with her."

Jeremy's core belief that he was not good enough on his own sabotaged his romantic relationships. His toxic productivity approach showed up in his romantic relationships by putting him on a timeline and making the stages of a relationship into a series of checklists he had to make his way through, instead of focusing on emotional connection. This was something Jeremy was not able to see right now, and the work we had to do was to help him identify this belief and how it affected his sense of self-worth.

Unlearning Old Core Beliefs to Make Space for New Ones

I like to remind my clients (and myself, at times) that anything learned can be unlearned. When we feel overpowered by situations, we can get stuck believing that we are destined to repeat the same experience over and over. Even when we realize that our situation is influenced by unhelpful thoughts and behaviors, the exhausting work of fighting those thoughts and behaviors can make us lose hope that anything will ever change. In fact, our real power to change our lives lies in changing our emotional world. Believing that you have the capability to unlearn and relearn your beliefs about yourself is a necessary first step in the journey of self-worth.

In Julia's case, her parents had not been able to provide an emotionally nurturing environment while she was growing up. She often felt rejected by her parents when she expressed any difficult emotions like sadness or anger. She was also shamed, criticized, and compared to others by her parents. This experience rooted a deep belief within her that something was inherently wrong with her, that she deserved less than she felt she needed.

As a result of this belief, any sign of conflict in her romantic relationships was evidence to Julia that her partner didn't really love her, that he would eventually leave her or simply continue to reject her.

This belief also showed up in her career as underselling herself. Instead of pursuing jobs that truly excited her or could elevate her career, she stuck to roles that were well below her skill and qualifications. Her belief was so strong that even in our session, she wasn't able to list any qualities or experiences that felt worthy of acknowledgment. Because her emotional world was still holding onto a story that told her *If I was enough on my own, I would have been loved by my parents when I was a child*, she was caught in a cycle of self-sabotage. To be enough, she felt she needed more devoted relationships, more powerful job titles, and more success, but whenever those things were within reach, her belief that she didn't deserve them caused her to retreat.

In one of our sessions, I gently asked, "What if nothing is wrong with you, Julia?"

She paused, seeming to consider this possibility for the first time. While she didn't have the answer that day, Julia was able, over time, to explore parts of herself that were unrelated to productivity and self-improvement. To transform her core beliefs about herself, Julia first had to identify each belief, examine the story she had constructed around it, and then reframe her perception to create a new core belief.

Exercise

Transforming Your Core Beliefs

Julia and I worked together on deconstructing her core beliefs over the course of many weeks. This exercise includes a series of reflection questions that she and I used for this work. Think through these questions and see if you can identify or even transform any core beliefs you have about yourself:

1. **Write down the story you currently believe:** If I was _____, then I would feel good enough.

   Example: *If I was more qualified, then I would feel good enough to be lovable.*

2. **Look for evidence for and against this thought.**

   Example: *For: If I was more successful, I'd match the rest of my family, which would make me more worthy of their love.*

   Against: My qualifications are one part of me, and there are more things about me that make me worthy of being loved, such as my kindness and sense of humor.

3. **Write down an alternative thought based on your reflections above.**

   Example: *I am worthy of being loved, as I am more than my qualifications.*

4. **Practice reminding yourself of this alternative thought regularly.**

Your Self-Worth Is Not Conditional

In scientific experiments, there are dependent and independent values. An independent value remains constant, meaning that it stays the same no matter what else changes in the experiment. A dependent value, on the other hand, changes when other experiment factors change.

Healthy self-worth functions as an independent value. When things change around you, such as a new relationship, a breakup, or a job loss, healthy self-worth ensures that your conviction of your inherent value stays the same. You see your worthiness as existing beyond the influence of external factors. However, when you see your self-worth as conditional, it functions as a dependent value in your life, fluctuating with every life event. Interestingly, this impacts your productivity as well: when your self-worth feels high, your productivity levels might plateau, but when your self-worth dips, your drive for productivity increases in an attempt to feel better about yourself.[21]

One of the biggest risks of conditional self-worth is that everyday failures and rejections begin to take on a deeper (and untrue) meaning. For instance, Julia shared one day that she had been recently laid off due to her employer closing its doors. Shortly after she got the news, she was in a taxi when the driver casually asked what she did for a living. This "small talk" question triggered her deep feeling of not being good enough. Over time, she was able to rationalize the situation and realize her worth as a human, apart from her job. Still, it became clear during our session that her pain was still lingering. She remained very anxious about the thought of going to a party or being on a date without a job to introduce herself with.

Sounds a lot like my story from the beginning of the chapter, doesn't it? Most people, especially the high achievers among us, can identify with this desire to be attached to something "bigger" than ourselves. It's normal to look to our jobs to give us a sense of identity, especially when we're just getting started in our lives as independent adults. Ideally, as we grow older, we develop relationships, interests, and ultimately, a deeper sense of self that makes us less dependent on our careers for identity. But for those with a dependent sense of self-worth, that broader identity never fully develops. Instead, we continue to depend on external markers of success as internal markers of worth, and sooner or later, this will inevitably lead to shame.

The remedy lies in attaching yourself to something bigger within you, instead of factors outside of you. Reflect on the parts of you (qualities, habits, characteristics, traits, etc.) that stay the same even when things around you change:

- Do you suddenly stop being a kind person if you lose your job?

- Do you lose your sense of humor if you didn't get that promotion?

- Are you a bad parent because a friend of yours buys a home while you are still renting?

Your rational answer is probably no. Like an independent value, your kindness, sense of humor, and skills as a parent are still very much intact. Your emotions, though, might not be so sure that this is the case. This is why it's important to cultivate a practice of regularly checking in with yourself.

Exercise

Your Self-Worth Is Not Tied to Your Productivity

Your productivity has no bearing on your worth. Use the following exercises to help you see your self-worth regardless of the things you get done:

- Practice introducing yourself, but do not talk about your job or the role you play in your family.

- Write a bio about yourself without including anything about your job or the role you play in your family.

- Write a list of things that make you feel worthy that have nothing to do with external achievements.

- Write a list of things about yourself that you value or are complimented on, that have nothing to do with productivity, status, or achievement.

Rebuilding Self-Worth Outside of Productivity

Some say life is random. I like to think life happens in seasons. No state of being is permanent; everything is cyclical. The same applies to the self-worth journey as well. Self-worth is not a constant trait—it ebbs and flows throughout our life.[22] Difficult life events in adulthood, such as failure, loss, or abandonment, may trigger familiar emotions and thoughts. Your self-worth will rise and fall over time as you ride the tide, dealing with the well-known pain and thriving in the moments of joy. Those who grew up with low self-worth can even be triggered by "good" life changes, like entering a new relationship, becoming a parent, or starting a new job; however, those whose families fostered high self-worth will also be internally impacted when life gets inevitably demanding.

It is undoubtedly easier to build self-worth back up if you have a good foundation, but you can learn to develop this skill through intention, self-awareness, and therapy. If you don't know where to begin, one small way to separate your self-worth from your productivity habits is to reframe the way you talk about productivity and self-worth. There are several practices you can adopt that will empower you to see yourself as worthy, regardless of your external circumstances, your past, or your thoughts:

- **Have accountability for your mistakes**, but do not shame yourself or put yourself down.
    - Original thought: *I am bad.*
    - Mindset shift: *I did a bad thing.*
- **Recognize failure as an event** instead of a personality trait.
    - Original thought: *I am a failure.*
    - Mindset shift: *I tried something and it failed.*
- **Detach material worth** from your personality.
    - Original thought: *Having nice things makes me better.*
    - Mindset shift: *I have nice things.*

- **Look at yourself as a whole person,** knowing that there are parts of you that are amazing and parts of you that you need to improve.
  - Original thought: *I am always right.*
  - Mindset shift: *I am sometimes wrong and sometimes right.*
- **Avoid comparisons to others;** instead, be inspired by them.
  - Original thought: *They have a better relationship than us.*
  - Mindset shift: *How can I improve my relationship so I feel good about it?*
- **Trust yourself** while also seeking other people's opinions on your decisions.
  - Original thought: *I need you to help me decide.*
  - Mindset shift: *This is what I decided; what do you think?*

Redefining Self-Worth

The more we raise our sense of self-worth, the less need we feel to increase our worth through toxic productivity. Disconnecting your self-worth from productivity begins with examining the core beliefs telling you that you deserve less than you need or that you'll only be enough when you've done enough.

There's no doubt that this inner work is challenging, and not only because it involves battling the brain's negativity bias. It's also difficult because it asks us to investigate past experiences that might be painful to revisit. This is why working on healthy self-worth is not a destination, but a journey. None of us arrive at healthy self-worth one day and stay there forever—it is a constant work-in-progress.

It is not easy to unlearn all the messages about achievement, productivity, and self-worth that we pick up along the way. It's even more difficult to relearn new, healthier ways of relating to success because of our hustle-obsessed culture that constantly preaches the myth that good things only happen to people who earn them.[23]

As you do the work of redefining your self-worth outside of what you produce or achieve, know that there will be times where you feel like you're going backward, as well as times when it feels a lot easier to revert to toxic productivity than to show up simply as who you are. Healing is not a linear process, and the practice of accepting yourself as you are can be tremendously scary. This is true even for the people you might assume have the highest self-worth. In her book *Becoming*, Michelle Obama recalls the self-doubt she felt as a young woman in high school surfacing years later when she became First Lady.[24] Even as one of the most successful women in the nation, she found herself asking once again, *Am I good enough?* But after years of overcoming obstacles, both external and within herself, she had developed the skill and the trust to counter her self-doubt by cultivating unconditional self-worth, allowing her to finally answer that question confidently: *Yes—I am enough.*

Key Takeaways

- Self-worth is an internal map of how you see yourself—specifically, if you feel "good enough" to feel a sense of belonging with others.

- Core beliefs are general principles that we have adopted about ourselves (internal) and the world (external).

- Toxic productivity habits become the way we attain a sense of worthiness, making it much easier to get trapped in the mindset that higher achievements will make us feel more worthy in our relationships.

- In order to transform unhelpful core beliefs about productivity and self-worth, we have to identify what we believe and then reframe our perception to create a new, more helpful core belief.

- Finding ways to lift your self-worth outside of productivity and achievement is an important part of healing and emotional growth.

Chapter 5

Managing Unresolved Shame

"There is no good or bad without us, there is only perception. There is the event itself and the story we tell ourselves about what it means."

—Ryan Holiday, *The Obstacle is the Way*

"I felt so different from everyone else. Everything about my family was different, you know?"

My friend Anna and I were sitting at the lobby bar of the Crosby Hotel in SoHo, sharing our childhood experiences over coffee and croissants. We were comparing the similarities and differences of how we grew up as children of South Asian immigrants.

Born and raised in the US, Anna was one of the few non-White students in her middle and high school classes. "I looked different; the way my parents spoke and dressed was never like the other parents; even my lunch was different," Anna recalled. "This always made me feel like I couldn't be a part of things unless I changed myself to become like the other—White—girls."

Here she paused, as if wondering if she should say what was on her mind. Slowly, she vocalized something that was evidently difficult for her to say out loud. "I felt so *ashamed* of being Brown."* Her pain and passion sounded fresh, even so many years later.

Listening to her, I was reminded of my own experiences with shame as a twelve-year-old Pakistani immigrant girl. On the surface our stories were different—while she was born in the US, I was born in Pakistan; she grew up in a totally White town while I grew up within an expat community in the Middle East and then immigrated to Toronto in my early teenage years. But at their core, our stories were the same.

As an adult, I have so much admiration for my parents and others who immigrate to foreign countries in hopes of better opportunities for themselves and their families. But at that time, twelve-year-old me hated it, and I was a brat about it. I didn't want to go to school, I didn't try to make friends with the neighborhood kids, and I was surly and broody. Everything was just *so* different in Toronto. I was not just the new kid; I was also the most different kid, not because everyone in the community was White (it was an immigrant community) but because nobody was like me. I spoke English with a slight accent, not poorly enough to be with the English-as-a-second-language kids but not as clearly as the native English speakers. I said I was Pakistani but had just arrived from Saudi Arabia, which was very confusing to the other kids in my class. They asked me if I "drove camels" to school and if I had to cover myself "in a black cloak." Nobody could say my name properly and everyone kept asking me what it meant; even the grown-ups stumbled with the pronunciation, making it awkward for everyone. Alienated by so much amazement at my very name, I hid in the bathroom during lunch for my entire first week. Being in Toronto felt like wearing an itchy sweater that was too big; the discomfort was impossible to ignore, and no matter how much I twisted and shifted, it never fit quite right.

---

* *Brown* is a common colloquial way of referring to yourself as South Asian.

One moment that stands out clearly in my memory happened on my second day of school in Canada. My teacher walked in, a bouncy blond ponytail high on her head and a clipboard in her hand. I knew she was about to take attendance, and I held my breath as she went down the list of students, my name quickly approaching. Her eyes widened slightly as she awkwardly paused in the middle of roll call—she'd certainly reached my name on the clipboard.

She struggled to say my name, but I raised my hand weakly in acknowledgment. After the teacher finished with the rest of the list, she looked over at me, asking me to step outside the classroom.

Feeling every single eye on me, I walked outside the classroom and into the empty hallway, palms sweating and eyes fixed on the tile floor. The teacher closed the door behind her and bent down to meet me at eye-level. "Honey, are you a boy or a girl?"

I stared blankly back at her, dumbfounded by such a bizarre question.

"Are . . . you . . . a BOY or GIRL?" she asked again, this time emphasizing all the syllables slower and louder than before.

She thought I didn't understand English, I realized. *Why is she asking me this? And why does she think I don't understand her?* I wanted to be back in my old classroom, with my old friends, more than ever.

"Uh, I'm a girl, miss," I managed to mumble, trying not to make eye contact, afraid she would see the beginnings of small tears.

The message was solidified: I did not belong there. I was someone so different that even the adults couldn't understand me. The way I looked, the foreignness of my name, my very identity ignited powerful emotions that I didn't quite understand at that time but remember so vividly even today.

Though I could have been offended by the other students or my teachers, it was *me* that I was ashamed of. The place was not wrong for me—I was wrong for it. Looking back at those moments now, I recognize those feelings as shame. It took me a long time to recognize that I continued to carry this shame with me long afterward.

The Connection Between Shame and Toxic Productivity

We can carry shame with us for years without realizing it. Sometimes, we don't even know what it looks like. Shame is a self-conscious emotion, meaning that it causes you to focus on yourself.[25, 26] It taps into primal fears of not being good enough to belong; in response, you do everything you can to fit in. It shouldn't be surprising, then, that shame feeds into the toxic productivity mindset. Shame urges us to use productivity habits and achievements to earn a sense of belonging. Shame also triggers intense emotions like embarrassment or sadness; to cope with these feelings, we often turn to avoidance.[27, 28] Avoidance behaviors naturally lead to feeling—sometimes accurately—like you have not done enough or are behind, which continues to feed into the toxic mindset.

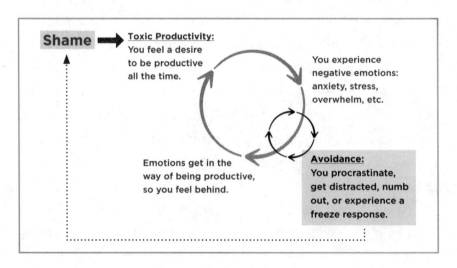

For instance, when I was writing this book and I came upon a section I was struggling to write, negative self-talk thoughts flooded my mind: *How can I get stuck writing about something I know so much about?* and *Everyone is going to realize I'm not a "real" writer.* When these thoughts set in, I would get up from my desk and start unnecessarily tidying up my closet, the kitchen pantry, or random parts of my house. I was being productive (though not in the way I needed to be at that moment) in an effort to distract myself from the shame I felt for being stuck in my writing.

Some other common avoidance strategies include:

- **Procrastinating** on a deadline because working on the project is too anxiety-provoking.

- **Numbing** yourself by using alcohol or other substances, eating, or passively binge-watching a show to dull the intensity of the emotion.

- **Overthinking or overpreparing** instead of doing what you're supposed to because thinking about it feels safer.

I hear about avoidance behaviors from my clients often. For example, Julia was ready to start the job search again. But no matter how often she tried, week after week, she still had not updated her résumé, which she needed to do to apply to new roles.

"Talk me through the moments leading up to you sitting down with your résumé last week," I asked.

"Okay." She took a deep breath. "I'd told myself that I would do it that night when I got home from work. I went for a workout, then I got back, showered, got a snack, and turned my laptop on to work on it . . . and then I ended up just staring at my document, not knowing what to write. So, then I thought I should do some research to get a better idea of what to write. I went onto Google to look at résumé samples, scrolled LinkedIn to see what people in my industry were saying on their résumé. I thought it would inspire me, but . . ." She trailed off. "Everyone I know seems like they've done so much, and I haven't."

"And then what did you do?"

"By then it was like 8:30 p.m., and I had to eat dinner. And then I just started watching TV." She sounded defeated.

I nodded along empathetically, knowing that state of mind all too well. I had been there many times myself—when applying to graduate school, looking for work, planning my wedding, writing this book. Julia's shame-based thoughts would initially motivate her to make a change, but as soon as she got started, they didn't allow her to go anywhere past the initial step. Looking for inspiration from others only made her feel more shame about herself in comparison, until the feeling grew unmanageable and moved her into avoidance.

"Let's examine the negative thoughts that came up when you sat down to edit your résumé," I proposed. I asked her to list her résumé-worthy achievements out loud.

She complied, but with very telling commentary. "Well, I got promoted last year, but I'm the oldest person on the team so the title doesn't look quite the same as it would if I were younger. I have a master's degree, and this role only requires a bachelor's. But I took so long to finish my degree, it probably doesn't count as much as someone else with a master's. I've brought in a large number of sales, but it doesn't feel like enough to be really impressive—everyone on my team makes sales."

Over and over, for every achievement she listed, she diminished its value by creating a caveat. She was shaming herself right in front of me.

"Julia, I can't help noticing that sometimes you're mean to yourself."

"I have to be mean to motivate myself," she said matter-of-factly. "It keeps me going."

I was struck by the bald honesty of her statement. "Why do you think that is?"

She looked at me like I had just asked a silly question. "This is how my mom did it with me," she replied plainly.

Throughout Julia's childhood, she explained, her mother criticized her for not doing anything right and for failing to match the accomplishments of her siblings. Wanting to prove to her mother that she was not a failure, Julia would work harder and take on more academic challenges and extracurricular activities. But under the weight of all these commitments, she would eventually lose steam, struggle to finish things, and ultimately abandon them. This cycle furthered her belief that she must keep doing more to prove to herself that she was not a failure, that she belonged among her siblings, the "good" kids in the family.

"How has this motivation technique worked out for you in past situations?" I asked.

"It helps me get out there and do things." She paused, then added, "Well, okay—it gets me to *start* things." She laughed wryly. "I guess I don't always finish the things I start."

"What do you think gets in the way of finishing things?"

"I get overwhelmed. Like you said, I'm being mean to myself and then start to feel bad. But it's always been hard for me to finish. My mom used to say I'm not a 'closer.'" Here, she took a sharp, deep breath and let it go with an exhausted sigh. I could see that this was painful for her to say out loud.

"And do you want to be a 'closer,' Julia?" I asked.

"Yeah, I do," she half-whispered. "I want to start something and finish it. I want to find a new job I can feel proud of. Instead of just *trying* to do something, I want to actually do something."

Together, Julia and I talked through other ways of finding motivation that were not shame-based so that her efforts didn't keep ending in avoidance and abandonment. But this conversation got me thinking: if shame *can* motivate us into some action, can there be a healthy way to use it? The answer is a bit complicated.

Does Shame Make You More Productive?

Getting motivation through shame is short-lived. Moreover, it is as unhealthy as it is unpleasant. Shame insists there is something inherently wrong with you, as opposed to your behavior or the situation. Unsurprisingly, shame-based motivation eventually translates into low self-worth.

If you met my friend Anna, you would never believe that she felt any shame about herself. She is a warm, confident, intelligent woman and has launched a very successful business within a span of just a few years. However, she has told me that she carried the childhood shame of being different for a long time. Moreover, she said that this shame was compounded throughout her life as she experienced the highs and lows of being an entrepreneur. Toxic productivity habits gave her a way to cope with that shame; achieving at the same level (or better) as the "normal" people temporarily made her feel less different from them.

"In a weird way, it was the feeling of not fitting in that really gave me the idea for my business," Anna told me. "I don't want anyone else to feel the way I did, just because of the way they look or the culture they are from. I wanted to show that there is a lot of power in being

South Asian, and just because I'm not a White American doesn't mean I don't belong here."

Like Julia, Anna also used shame as motivation. Building a business based on her culture was Anna's way of saying "I belong." But while shaming herself to be more productive *did* sometimes yield the outcome she desired, it came at a personal cost.

"It was exhausting to keep fighting the urge to keep doing more," she told me. "Nothing ever permanently made me feel like I'd done enough to prove I belong. I felt like I had no choice but to keep building. Eventually, nothing I did made me feel good."

The shame of potentially failing, of disappointing others, of letting down her younger self who had tried so hard to fit in, led Anna to overidentify with productivity, to focus on her business goals at the expense of everything else in her life. Eventually, her tunnel vision on productivity caused her to make rash decisions, and her lack of motivation impacted the company culture. In the end, she even became so physically sick that she had to take time off from work.

"That was a wake-up call for me," Anna remembered. "My body had to shut down to show me that this way of living was not sustainable. I realized I had to look inward and figure out a new way to be productive, for the sake of my own health."

"It sounds like you had become disconnected from yourself at some point," I said. "What brought you back?"

"I'm close with my chief operating officer, and she told me I needed a place to 'feel out loud,' so I started therapy."

Anna realized in therapy that she was being driven by a subconscious desire to correct the shame she'd felt in her childhood. The desperation to get rid of this shame led her to abandon her emotional and physical needs. Before she could figure out a way to transform her motivation into something healthier and sustainable, she had to first investigate the roots of her shame, to delve into her first experiences of it and the foundation of what she understood as shameful.

Where Does Productivity Shame Come From?

In chapter 2, we talked about how our core beliefs are largely formed in childhood by the lessons we are taught and our observations of things happening around us. These lessons and observations shape our ideas about the world, who we are and, perhaps more importantly, who we should aim to become and who we should avoid becoming. These are known as the *wanted identity* (how we want others to perceive us) and the *unwanted identity* (how we don't want others to perceive us).[29,30,31,32]

The wanted identity leads us to develop a set of traits and habits that we believe will help us fit in and make us feel connected to others—in other words, provide that sense of belonging that is a basic emotional need. Oftentimes, the better we match up to our wanted identity, the more we increase our self-esteem. Conversely, anytime we embody the traits of our unwanted identity, we feel shame and fear that we might be rejected.

Our wanted identities can be built in a number of ways—most often we aim to "match" or fit in with the people around us. This includes, in our early days, our caregivers, siblings, extended family, and friends. As we grow older, we are introduced to more identities, through social media, advertisements, our careers, or our friend groups. In order to feel that sense of belonging, we unconsciously start to craft a wanted identity that will help us fit in, and the more we embody this, the better we feel. This, of course, can also include identities that put high pressure on success, achievement, and productivity.

Our wanted identities can also be created in response to an unwanted identity, often unconsciously. For instance, my parents' experiences in the strict social hierarchy of 1970s Bangladesh fostered a belief that simply being good at your job wasn't good enough to advance professionally. As Brown people working within a predominantly White environment, they believed that the burden of proof rested with them—if they didn't prove their value with hard work, they would risk being replaced. This mindset carried over from the workplace to our household; I grew up in a family where rest was not modeled. I rarely saw my parents sleeping in on weekends or lying on the couch to watch TV for an evening. There was always something going on, somewhere to go, some household errand to catch up on—all of it in response to the unwanted identity of being idle.

I felt this same pressure, and it was hardly a lesson I needed to be sat down and taught. Any activity that could be associated with idleness made me feel like I didn't belong in my family and consequently activated feelings of shame. This impacted my behavior throughout childhood, setting habits in place that continued long after I left home. As an adult, I avoided resting, watching Netflix, shopping as a leisure activity, or doing anything that might indicate to others that I was being unproductive. I also pursued a staggering number of activities and commitments in order to feel like I was someone who was productive, all to avoid feeling shame. That lasted until I, like Anna, hit the dead end of burnout.

Shame is difficult to identify because we learn to hide it through coping mechanisms, such as avoidance or denial. Over time, those coping mechanisms become so second nature that we can forget all about the shame that drives them. But the shame, and the wound that created it, still lives underneath. What I had never realized was how much shame I was still carrying from early experiences.

I didn't come to this realization on my own. (If only life was that easy!) It happened during one of my own therapy sessions. I was telling my therapist about a past manager of mine who made discriminatory comments about my cultural and religious heritage in front of me and other colleagues. The whole thing was confusing. I couldn't figure out why he had no consequences, why I didn't react to him, or what emotions I was feeling.

"I was so angry, I totally froze. I couldn't believe he was *actually* saying what he was saying," I ranted indignantly to my therapist. "It's like he didn't even care that I was sitting right there as he belittled Muslims. It didn't matter. *I* didn't matter."

Of course, my therapist agreed with how disrespectful this whole thing was. She let me vent for a few minutes, and once she felt like I had gotten it off my chest, she finally said, "I know you are angry and offended, as you should be. Can you think about how you felt immediately in the moment when he said what he said?"

I took a deep breath and begrudgingly named the feeling I had been trying to ignore ever since the incident. It had been floating in my mind for a few days, but I had been avoiding it.

"It made me think, *I am not good enough to be in this room right now because of who I am.* Which is ridiculous. He's the one who did something wrong, but I was the one feeling bad about myself."

"What did you think you should do about it?" she asked.

"What I did and what I think I should have done are different. The weeks following that event, I started working extra hard, you know? Trying to prove that I do belong, that I am a good worker. I took on a lot of work. What I should have done is told him to screw off with his bigoted nonsense or, like, filed a complaint against him!"

My manager's comments about my heritage had activated my unwanted identity: someone for whom being good at your job isn't good enough. Just like my parents, I felt that I had to prove my value or risk being replaced, only this instance went deeper—his comments not-so-subtly implied that I would never be good enough, that no amount of hard work could compensate for a cultural heritage he saw as less-than.

In hindsight, I see that my response to my manager's actions may not have been my best option, but at that time I went into hyper-productivity mode to prove that I was good enough, regardless of his bigoted opinion. However, through my own self-discovery work, I had finally started to examine the shame that had been motivating me for so long.

Transforming Your Productivity Shame into Something More Helpful

We can start to navigate our feelings of shame by bringing them out in the open and examining them. This was the only way I learned about the types of thoughts I was carrying with me, and how they showed up in my beliefs and productivity habits. In the following exercises, we will explore your shame narrative and how you can transform it into something healthier and more constructive.

Exploring Your Shame Narrative

One way to change your relationship with shame is to question the narrative you believe about it. You might already know it, or the answer might surprise you. I encourage you to be kind yet honest with yourself. I've included an example from my own life to guide you through the exercise. Use the following exploration to expand on your shame narrative:

Step 1: **Reflect** on what stories you believe to be true about productivity. Then think about how you adapt your behavior to match it.

- I believe people who (1) _____ (action/behavior) are (2) _____ (trait/label/judgment).

- I want people to see me as (3) _____ , (trait/label/judgment), so I do (4) _____ (action/behavior) and avoid (5) _____ (action/behavior).

Example:

- *I believe women who **rest** are **lazy**. I want people to see me as **ambitious and hard-working**, so I use my evenings to **take courses** and avoid **bingeing Netflix**.*

Step 2: Next, let's **connect** with your feelings about this story.

- Take a look at what you wrote for (2). What do you feel if you imagine that people see you like this?

  ○ *If people see me as lazy, I feel uncomfortable and disgusted.*

- Review your answers for (4) and (5). How do you feel about the actions/behavior you engage in and the ones you avoid?

  ○ *When I am taking courses, I feel better about myself— I know more so I can speak confidently at parties.*

  ○ *I feel a little embarrassed for not knowing the TV shows people are talking about.*

Step 3: Now, let's **question** this story.

- Where did I learn these ideas about how people should be?

  - *I was raised to believe that the "idle hands are the devil's workshop." I also understood that many people don't have the opportunities I have, which meant I'd be wasting my privilege by not making the most of it. All the people I admire are people who work hard. And anyway, we can rest when we're older.*

- Look again at what you wrote for (5). What would happen if you did the things you avoid?

  - *I would get a chance to take a break and feel a little less stressed. I would get to spend some quality time with my partner. I would also feel a little guilty.*

- If your friend was living according to this story, what would you say to them?

  - *I would say: I think it's great you take courses and classes all the time, but it would be good for you to relax a little. You're stressed out a lot of the time.*

Step 4: Finally, let's see how we can flip the script. Can you **transform** this story?

- I see myself as (1) _____ (trait/label/judgment), even when I am doing (5) _____ because _____ .

  - *I see myself as **hard-working**, even when **I take a break or watch Netflix for an evening**, because that **helps me rest and recharge**, so I can keep learning and becoming better at what I love.*

Once you can identify and recognize your shame narrative, you can transform it into curiosity. Turning the self-judging, shame-based thoughts into self-directed curiosity gives you the opportunity to look at your beliefs, reframe them, and break the toxic productivity mindset.

Taking Your Shame from Judgment to Curiosity

If you think about what shame sounds like in your head, you might notice that it resembles a familiar voice or that it makes you feel like you're back in a place or time you wish you could forget. Shame is essentially a repeat of our past experiences of being criticized or judged by someone else. Only now, the judgment is coming directly from you instead of another person.

One of the things that makes shame so tricky to work through is that it sometimes draws on valid critiques. We all have unhelpful habits to work on and times when we fail to show up as our best selves. This is normal. We're only human, after all. The problem arises when a valid critique of something you've done is internalized as a judgment of who you are as a person. Perhaps you had a parent, teacher, or coach who rightly pointed out that you weren't applying yourself, but wrongly framed it in terms of your character: "You're lazy," "You have no work ethic," "You'll never get ahead in life if you expect to ride other people's coattails." This sets you up for hearing any and all feedback, including your own thoughts, as judgments of who you are and what you're capable of.

Fortunately, as adults we can learn to reverse this by transforming shame's judgments into curiosity. Where shame makes you feel powerless to change, curiosity empowers you to become compassionately aware of what is holding you back and find intelligent, effective ways to break through it.

Transforming Shame Into Curiosity

Transforming shame into curiosity is the way to take your power back from the messages you were told in childhood. Use the following strategies to become curious about how you feel shame. For each strategy, see if you can think of a shame statement you've had, and shift the statement to be more self-reflective:

- **Rephrase black-and-white beliefs about yourself into open-ended questions:** Absolute statements don't have space for nuance and are closed to the potential for change. In reality, we experience a lot of nuances and are always changing.

  - Original thought: *I'll never be a good employee.*

  - Mindset shift: *What needs to change in my life for me to feel like a good employee?*

  - What is a black-and-white shame thought you've had about yourself? Can you change your mindset and shift this thought?

- **Refrain from overgeneralizing about yourself:** If you are using words like *always* and *never* to describe yourself, stop and ask yourself how true those descriptions are.

  - Original thought: *I'm a high-strung person.*

  - Mindset shift: *What are some situations I'm more relaxed in? Which places am I more high-strung in? Is there a pattern?*

  - What is an overgeneralizing shame thought you've had about yourself? Can you change your mindset and shift this thought?

- **Do not believe everything you think about yourself:** Many of the self-beliefs you have were taught to you, either through experiences or things adults told you when you were a child. How many of them are still true and helpful?

  - Original thought: *I'm just a slow learner.*

- ◦ Mindset shift: *I learn differently than others.*
- ◦ Have you learned anything about yourself in the past that still brings you shame in the present? Can you change your mindset and shift this thought?

Reclaim Your Identity from Shame

Remember that the driving force behind the toxic productivity mindset is the desire to feel good enough about yourself to believe that you belong. When a person or situation activates a toxic mindset in you, it's safe to assume that shame is lurking at the bottom of it all. For Anna, the shame came from feeling different, even from those in her own community. For Julia, it was the feeling of being inferior to the rest of her family. For me, it was the feeling that my racial and ethnic heritage left me with something to prove.

What I hope all three stories show is that shame is fundamentally based on a lie. That it is possible to reclaim your identity and power without resorting to shame or toxic productivity. Shame sets in when you take personal responsibility for something that is happening outside of you; it tells you that something is wrong with you, not the situation or circumstance you are in. Whether it happens through socialization, family dynamics, culture, or community, it's vital to recognize that shame is never warranted or justified. Most of the time, it's a tool used by those in power to maintain their status by keeping other people focused on their own shortcomings instead of the shortcomings of the situation. But even when it's used by people who love and care for us, shame prevents the very solution it's intended to offer. Being critical and harsh toward yourself keeps you from really understanding yourself and learning how you can improve.

Improving any area of life begins with building self-awareness through curiosity, compassion, and confidence. This is not an overnight fix—as the stories in this chapter show, dismantling shame is a deep inner journey that is challenging and takes time. Remember, you're never going to overcome shame by shaming yourself into it. In fact, the most effective way to conquer shame is to take the process slowly. This is how we gain power over our shame.

Key Takeaways

- Shame drives toxic productivity through two powerful thought patterns that work together: (1) Nothing you do ever feels enough, and (2) everything you do has to be in the service of becoming "enough." As a result, you feel compelled to do productive things and avoid "time-wasting" activities.

- What we often don't realize is that, behind the scenes, shame is operating both to activate toxic productivity through increasing the desire to do more and maintain it through avoidance behavior.

- Shame doesn't make you productive, even if the emotional pain of shame can mask itself as motivation.

- If our wanted identity (how we want people to see us) is to be productive, we may become stuck in the toxic productivity mindset to avoid an unwanted identity (how we don't want others to see us).

- One powerful way to unlearn shame is transforming your shame into curiosity. This makes it more manageable, helpful, and less painful.

Chapter 6

When Everything Must Be Perfect

"The fact that you are imperfect is not a sign that you have failed;
it is a sign that you are human, and more importantly, it is a
sign that you still have more potential within you."

**—Brianna Wiest, *The Mountain Is You: Transforming
Self-Sabotage Into Self-Mastery***

A weird energy permeated the therapy room. So, I did what I do best:
I named it.

"What's up, Lara?" I asked. "I may be wrong—correct me if so—
but you seem a bit on edge today?"

Silence.

"Is there something you feel like you want to share or something I
said that didn't sit well with you from a previous session?"

More silence. *I'm going to let this silence settle in, let her meet me here,*
I thought to myself.

After a few moments, Lara rummaged through her purse
distractedly, avoiding direct eye contact with me.

"Ah, there it is." She fished her lip balm from some inner corner in
her bag. "I was thinking about what you said last week, that I should
think about how the things I do make me feel. I did think about it,

and . . ." She looked away again, then blurted out, "The thing is, they make me feel good." She waved her hands around, pointing to herself. "I, uh . . . I don't want to change this part of me."

Many people believe that therapists want to change them. That couldn't be further from the truth. A therapist holds up a mirror for you to see yourself, your life, and your habits more clearly so that you can become more aware of your patterns and *choose* what you want to change.

"What part don't you want to change?" I prompted.

"That I get so much done," she answered, speaking rapidly. "And I get it all done right. You know the phrase 'Done is better than perfect'? My version of that is 'Done equals perfect.' I'm always striving for the things I do to be at the highest level. Why wouldn't anyone want that? Being this way is what made me successful." She glanced at me, as if to assess whether or not I was on her side.

It's not unusual for people in therapy to become protective of the very things that are disrupting their lives. Our brains are wired to instinctively see change as a threat; even if our current habits, patterns, or mindset are causing some sort of issue (and even if we're aware of this issue), there's a certain kind of comfort in what's familiar.

"I see what you're saying. I wouldn't want to change myself either, especially if what I'm doing seems to be working," I assured Lara. "I wonder though, can you look at your habits and your self as separate from each other?"

She looked at me thoughtfully. "I don't know what that means. How can I be different from my habits?"

This comment was very illuminating—it revealed Lara's belief that ensuring things were perfect wasn't something she did, but rather who she was. Lara felt she had only two choices: be perfect at everything or be someone else entirely. No wonder she was resistant to change!

What Is Perfectionism?

Perfectionism, the aspiration toward flawlessness in everything we do, is the rare behavioral dysfunction that we talk about as though it's a craft, or even a vocation.[33] Calling someone a perfectionist is often as much a compliment as it is a critique. When someone refers to themselves as a perfectionist, there's a note of "sorry not sorry" about it. The implication is that we'd all be perfectionists if we had the strength, intelligence, and tenacity to produce flawless outcomes in everything we do.

It just so happened that Lara did have all those qualities. And her vision of an ideal life wasn't that different from her husband's—a successful career, a loving and committed relationship, kids who were healthy and thriving. So why was her marriage struggling? It was her individual interpretation of that vision that was causing some problems. What her husband saw as too many time commitments was, for Lara, a requisite part of succeeding in her career and helping their kids thrive. More than that, it was a natural expression of who she understood herself to be. To be a good employee, she had to be the perfect employee. To be a good mother, she had to be a perfect mother. As she herself said, everything had to be done at the highest level. She didn't want to be the best in comparison to others—she wanted to be the best it was possible to be. That goal, however, made it impossible for her to negotiate their family's busy lifestyle with her husband. While she was invested in her marriage enough to attend therapy, the idea of loosening her standards felt like a compromise of who she was as a person.

It could be argued that her husband was the one who needed to change, to raise his standards to Lara's level. It could also be that neither of them should have to change, that their differing interpretations of their shared vision simply made them incompatible as partners.

However, research shows that perfectionists tend to secretly suffer from painful flaws in their inner life, characterized by:[34, 35, 36]

- **Setting unrealistic goals:** While having high standards sounds good in theory, in practice, it typically results in asking more from yourself than is humanly possible to fulfill. Not only does this tend to create unhealthy imbalances in your life where you devote too much time to a relationship or a job at the expense of your own needs, but it also breeds an expectation of reciprocity from others. This leads you to become outraged if a friend doesn't return your call immediately or if your coworkers don't agree to pull an all-nighter with you.

- **Having excessive concerns about avoiding mistakes:** Expecting yourself to get it right the first time, every time, tends to provoke disproportionate reactions when human error or life's unpredictability get in your way. In relationships, this might look like being extremely cautious to avoid conflict. In the workplace, it might look like micromanaging your team members or taking on other people's work to ensure it gets done "right."

- **Needing others to recognize and appreciate your efforts:** Overdelivering on what was asked or expected from you might seem like a great way to show someone (boss, partner, friend, etc.) how much you care, but it tends to create a proportionate need for them to focus on you. For example, if you planned the company retreat or a friend's bridal shower, instead of letting people simply enjoy the experience, you might find yourself feeling resentful if they aren't giving you enough credit or if (God forbid) they find things to criticize about the experience.

- **Feeling an irrational sense of vulnerability:** Expecting yourself to be the best version of anything—the best employee, the best partner, the best friend, the best family member—warps your interpretation of other people's actions. Seeing a photo of your friend spending time with someone else, for example, might provoke thoughts like "What did I do wrong? Why did they ask that person to hang out instead of me?" Even when there are no reasons at all for concern, perfectionism can lead to rumination and self-sabotaging behaviors, such as "It's been a couple of days since we talked—I'd better check in. If I'm not the ideal friend, they might drop me for someone better."

- **Being unable to handle critique or disagreement:** The intense vulnerability that comes as a side effect of perfectionism makes any feedback that is less than glowing feel like a personal attack. Even when you accept (in theory) that someone has the right to disagree with you, you may often find yourself resenting them for not seeing things from your perspective—after all, as the one who clearly cares the most, don't you deserve to have the final say?

Much like toxic productivity, perfectionism is a bid for the acceptance and approval of others.[37] The belief goes something like this: *If I am perfect, or at least if I try hard enough to be perfect, then everyone in my life will love and accept me, and I will have "solved" any potential problems in my life before they even come up.* But as the previous list shows, perfectionism by its very nature ends up creating the problems it is intended to solve.

The thing is, perfectionists tend to be very intelligent and socially attuned people. In the end, most of us catch onto the fact that our attempts to be perfect are ultimately sabotaging our own goals. So why do we keep doing it, even when we know better?

Where Does Perfectionism Come From?

Like shame-based motivation (which we discussed in chapter 5), perfectionism is something we learn. Perfectionism is a mix of unrealistic standards, not being able to handle mistakes, and the need to be accepted by others, and this framework develops early in life. According to one of the leading researchers on perfectionism, Thomas Curran, if our emotional needs of attachment (connection) and self-worth are unmet, we learn to compensate with perfectionism, seeking a sense of belonging from our caregivers and eventually in other relationships as well.[38]

So, how did Lara make the connection between belonging, productivity, and perfectionism? To find the answer, we had to go back to the beginning.

Lara grew up in a volatile household, and her parents often argued with each other. Though her parents had their own interpersonal issues, they weaponized their children in their arguments, blaming each other for any mistakes their children made.

As we were talking about childhood memories that stood out, Lara began sharing her thoughts from that time in her life. She had recently found an old diary from when she was ten years old. In an even tone, she began reading:

Dear Diary, today at dinner, Dad asked about the geography test. I told him I got a B. He got angry at me, and then at Mom. He was saying if she wasn't so busy with her friends and TV shows, then I'd be doing better at school. This made Mom upset, and she started yelling at him, and he got up from the dinner table and went outside. I don't know where he went. Mom started to cry and said she wished I didn't make her look bad all the time. I told her I knew she was trying to be the best mom. I told her I would try harder next time. I am trying. I wish my parents didn't fight all the time. I wish I didn't get a B. Maybe Mom and Dad wouldn't fight with each other or be angry with me. Maybe today's dinner would have been nice, like the dinners at Sandy's house. Her parents don't fight, and they smile at each other. I never see Mom and Dad smile at each other.

She stopped there, smiled at me with pain in her eyes, and said, "I wish I could tell my ten-year-old self that people will love you no matter what, but I guess I don't believe that, even as an adult."

"Thank you for reading that out loud; I know it was difficult for you to revisit those moments," I said, knowing that this was probably one of the few times she had verbalized these feelings.

You can see how, by pulling Lara into their arguments and using her behaviors against each other, Lara's parents cemented the idea in her mind that the people she loved would be happier (and argue less) if she did not make any mistakes. That belief became a core narrative in her life, and as an adult, it showed up in all her relationships: friendships, romantic, and work-related.

Even though she no longer lived with her parents, the echoes of those experiences were still guiding her choices. This is also why she internalized her achievements as an extension of her identity. Being so closely attached to achievements, she became intolerant of mistakes and was unable to see her own value outside of what she could do. With this core narrative came a set of behaviors: difficulty saying no, overcommitting, and devaluing rest.

Exercise

What Does Perfectionism Mean to You?

Reflect on the following questions to consider whether your relationship with productivity is healthy or if it is consumed by perfectionism:

- Do your standards help you achieve your goals, or do they get in the way?

- Are your personal standards higher than those other people hold for you?

- Do you get overly upset if you or someone else can't measure up to your standards?

- Would relaxing some of those rules or standards you set for yourself save you time or energy? Would it offer any other benefits?

How Perfectionism Impacts Your Productivity

As you can probably guess, perfectionism and toxic productivity go hand in hand. Like shame, perfectionism brings qualities that could hypothetically foster productivity: relentless work ethic, high standards, and no space for mistakes or half-measures. As Lara put it, "Done means perfect." In reality, though, perfectionism runs counter to productivity. Equating "done" with "perfect" ends up breeding a few distinct behaviors that get in the way of doing anything at all. I'll explain each behavior in detail in the next sections. As you read through them, consider if and when any of them show up for you and how each impacts the way you feel.

Procrastination

Procrastination happens when you must do something on a deadline, but you delay doing it until the last minute. This can lead to doing things haphazardly, and you might even fail to meet the deadline altogether. All the while, you are aware of the looming deadline, but continue to put off the tasks.

As counterintuitive as it sounds, procrastination is a very common byproduct of perfectionism. In the perfectionism mindset, you might put off what you have to do because you fear that you won't complete it perfectly. The desire for flawlessness creates self-doubt and anxious thoughts that keep you from attempting what you need to do. This keeps you stuck in toxic productivity because by procrastinating you contribute to the feeling of being behind, which further pushes you deeper into the desire of needing to do more.

If you struggle with procrastination, one small change you can make to the way you approach things is to break a large task into multiple, smaller ones. This will help you learn to focus on the process, not just the results. It will also help you feel a sense of achievement as you complete the smaller tasks. Over time, if you begin to develop the mindset of "process over progress" or making space for achievements, you will be able to break out of the perfectionist mindset.

Black-and-White Thinking

Black-and-white thinking is a rigid mindset that evaluates the things you do as being binary—complete versus incomplete, perfect versus imperfect, good versus bad. Black-and-white thinking has no space for nuance. When things are either complete or incomplete in your mind, you can't celebrate any progress. This keeps you stuck within a toxic mindset because nothing feels good enough until it is done perfectly.

If you struggle with black-and-white thinking, one small change you can make to the way you approach things is to cultivate the skill of being in the present moment. The perfectionist mindset will urge you to focus on the results only; being present will force you to focus on the moment you are in now. By being present, you will be able to acknowledge the progress in the middle space and appreciate the small wins as they happen.

Impostor Syndrome

Impostor syndrome is the pervasive feeling of not being deserving of your accomplishments or being afraid that others will discover that you are not qualified or good enough at what you do. This feeling perpetuates the need to be perfect. Behind this is a lot of self-doubt—people who struggle with perfectionism and impostor syndrome question their abilities, which compels them to continue working harder to try to meet the unrealistic expectations set by their perfectionist attitudes. In a nutshell, the more you feel like a fraud, the more you commit to doing more to prove to others that you *are* deserving and not a fraud. This continues to feed the toxic productivity mindset.

If you struggle with impostor syndrome, one small change you can make to the way you approach things is to reframe critical self-talk to a more balanced and compassionate version. Transforming self-criticism into healthy self-talk helps reduce self-doubt, breaking the toxic mindset. Another thing you can do is to keep a list of all the things *you* know you have succeeded at, no matter how big or small. This will serve as a reminder that you are not an impostor, especially when the self-doubt shows up.

Aim for Your Best, Not Perfection

Like most aspects of toxic productivity, perfectionism causes you to think you are deficient in some way, which creates anxiety that others will notice this deficiency in you. In response, you may end up spending a lot of time courting others' approval by changing something about yourself so they view you a certain way and you feel a sense of belonging.

When we are in a toxic mindset, any threat to perfectionism is a threat to the potential of achievement, which in turn is a threat to belonging. This is why we hold on to perfectionist ideals, even when they are causing disruption in our lives. The belief that perfection is the panacea to your struggles is so powerful that people can no longer see the damage it creates in their life.

Breaking out of the perfectionist mindset requires distinguishing between excellence and perfection. Those who struggle with perfectionism are interested in only the outcome of their process, value efficiency over effort, and feel like none of their work is worthwhile unless the outcome is perfect the first time. Those invested in excellence enjoy the craft and problem-solving involved in their process, value learning along the way, and give themselves credit making for progress toward their goal. Another name for this approach is called *excellencism* instead of perfectionism, a distinction coined by social scientist and psychology professor Patrick Gaudreau.[39] Excellencism means reframing your mindset from "Everything I do must be perfect" to "Everything I do, I do my best at." What's the difference between the two? When we aspire for perfection, our thinking is rigid and we are unable to adapt or respond creatively to new information or opportunities. When we aspire to excellence, there is flexibility in how we approach our work and assess the results.

Of course, for someone like Lara, who has always seen doing her best as doing things perfectly, the distinction must be even more subtle. Therefore, to understand if your need to succeed has become toxic, it requires deep reflection into the intention of your actions: are your efforts intended to satisfy what someone has asked of you or are they intended to influence what someone thinks or feels about you? Said in another way: do your efforts excite you and give you confidence, or are they being done only to avoid a perceived threat?

Can You Be a Beginner?

I was sitting in the park one spring day, people-watching and eating a croissant, when I found myself watching this toddler attempt to walk toward a bush of flowers. He took two wobbly steps, then fell. Then he got up again, tried the same way, and fell again. This happened a few times until he reached the flowers. He wasn't focused on how or why he fell, who was watching him, or all the obstacles between him and the flowers. He simply got up after a fall and tried again. Once he got the flower, he happily wobbled back toward his stroller.

I couldn't help by wonder, *Why do adults become so afraid of falling?* Think about it—how many times have you not attempted something because you thought you would suck at it? How many opportunities have you passed on because you were afraid of failing?

That's one of biggest things Maya struggled with—feeling stuck in her life and not able to break out of the idea of the "perfect timeline" for her life's milestones. She felt like she had stagnated in her career over the past few years, and she was now mulling over applying for a more senior role or leaving her job altogether. However, she continued to shy away from anything that was new, different, or outside of her comfort zone. Not wanting to feel like a beginner prevented her from trying anything that would change her situation.

To break out of the echo chamber, we must dare to be a beginner. One way to start building a beginner's mindset is to reflect on the beliefs you hold about trying new things. What do you tell yourself about trying new things? The next time you come across a new experience, see if you can adopt a beginner's mindset by asking yourself these questions: *What if this is a learning exercise? What can I learn from this experience, even if it doesn't go as planned?*

That's what Maya had to do—choose between risking failure or staying the same. The idea of moving to a new role was too uncomfortable for her. She was afraid of applying to new roles, for fear of not getting them. At the same time, she was heavily criticizing herself for not making it into a more senior leadership position in her current role.

"What do you think you need to feel more confident in applying to this new role?" I asked. She had just shared that a new role in a different department had opened, and she was interested.

"I don't know if I meet all the criteria. It'll be a large team to manage, and I've only ever managed smaller teams of five or so. Plus, I don't know everything about that new role, the people, the department . . ." She listed all the reasons for not applying.

"You'd have to become a beginner in some ways in this new role, then?" I asked.

"Yes, well, partly . . . yeah. I know some of the things. It just feels weird to apply to a job where I don't meet all the criteria. I think by next year, maybe I'll have all the criteria met and then I can start thinking about it."

Being a beginner means stepping out of your comfort zone into something new and unknown. It means being comfortable with making mistakes. It requires mental flexibility to step out of the black-and-white thinking. It means reminding yourself that it's okay to be bad at something, that it doesn't mean it's not worth pursuing. This was the work Maya and I had to do together.

I decided to challenge her. "You've been in the role for almost four years and have continuously aced your reviews. You've stepped into managing larger teams in the interim as some colleagues took parental leave or vacations. What makes you think you need to learn something *more?*"

"I'm just not ready yet, I think. Of course, I want to move up and just move on with things in my life. I know, I just don't know if it's something . . . I don't know," she replied.

"Maybe next time we can talk through some of the thoughts you're having that might be holding you back," I said, hopeful it would sow a seed in her mind.

In our next session, she told me that she'd decided not to pursue the role. Coming to terms with perfectionism and the toxic productivity mindset is a slow journey, and Maya wasn't there yet. We would continue to work on making small changes in her habits. While Maya was exasperated with herself, she wasn't yet at the point where the discomfort of remaining the same outweighed the fear of changing.

In a world that values expertise, we are embarrassed to be beginners. At some point, usually by the end of college, we stop trying to learn new things. We become focused on being an expert in one thing and build the rest of our life to support that expertise. But we were all beginners at one point. When we allow ourselves to step outside the safety of expertise and risk the vulnerability of being a beginner again, we open ourselves up to possibilities we may never have imagined.

Key Takeaways

- Perfectionism encourages you to do things "perfectly" as a way to be more productive; it also leads to a fear of mistakes or an unwillingness to even start something new.

- We learn to connect perfectionism with our sense of belonging early in life, believing that being flawless will gain love and acceptance from our caregivers.

- Perfectionism leads to three habits that keep you locked in toxic productivity: procrastination, black-and-white thinking, and impostor syndrome.

- Reflect on your *why*—should you complete tasks because you need to satisfy what someone has asked of you or because it gives you confidence?

- A way out of perfectionism is to focus on the process instead of the outcomes, build mental flexibility, and learn to accept mistakes and flaws as part of the process.

Chapter 7

Comparing Yourself to Others

"Comparison is an act of violence against the self."

—Iyanla Vanzant, *Forgiveness: 21 Days to Forgive Everyone for Everything*

"Her life is going so well. How am I so behind?"

"His relationship seems so perfect; all we do is fight."

"Their house is always so *damn* clean. I can't even keep the sink free of dishes."

"Everyone else I know has a master's degree; I'll never be as smart as them."

Do any of these thoughts sound familiar? If so, you're not alone. Comparing yourself to others is normal human behavior. According to some studies, 10–12 percent of your daily thoughts involve some level of social comparison, or measuring parts of your life against another person's.[40]

Some of the most common ways we compare ourselves to others include:

- **Finances:** How much money we make, savings we have, what we can afford

- **Physical appearance:** How we look (body shape, size, weight, etc.),[41] how we dress and groom ourselves, our level of attractiveness

- **Relationships:** Relationship status, quality of relationships, children, activities, number of friends

- **Opportunities:** Travel, lifestyle, career, social activities

Interestingly, we tend to compare ourselves the most to people who are like us in some way. This can help us expand our ideas of what is possible—when a goal has been proved achievable by someone like us, it feels more achievable to us. But comparison can also have a limiting effect. Instead of pursuing goals we authentically value, comparison subtly influences us to channel our energy into matching the achievements or life paths of our peer group in order to—what else?—fit in.

The Comparing Mind

Sarah was extremely passionate about her job and had stable friendships and close relationships with her family. But she still struggled to feel like she was doing enough, making it difficult to feel connected with her friends, whom she viewed as being more successful and settled than her.

Sarah started one of our sessions by sharing a recent encounter with one of her closest friends. "Yasmin is one of my oldest friends, but the last few times we've hung out, I feel like I'm faking it."

"I know you've mentioned before that you've started to dread hanging out with her," I replied. "I wonder if you can name the emotions you have after you leave?"

"Honestly . . ." She hesitated, pulling at the frayed threads on her sweater's sleeves. "I hate to say it, but I feel so drained. I can't stop thinking about how our lives turned out so differently. Every time I meet her, she is doing something that just reminds me of how far behind I am."

"Tell me more about that," I said. I could see she was weighed down by something she needed to get off her chest.

Sarah took a deep breath. "She—no, *all* of my friends are 'doing life' better than me. Yasmin has a way higher-paying job than me. In fact, just a few months ago she got promoted. She owns a home. She travels all the time. All these guys like her—we can't go to a party without her leaving with someone's number."

I nodded, encouraging her to go on.

"And I'm happy for her, of course," Sarah quickly added, "but I don't know if I fit in with her anymore, especially with how different our income is. I . . . I just can't be myself anymore, you know?" She trailed off into silence.

I let that silence sit between us. Where I used to rush to fill an awkward silence with words—observations, validation, sometimes even a quote that fits the situation—I now know that in this silence, people are often forced to confront what they have been avoiding.

Sure enough, after a few moments, Sarah half-whispered another reflection. "I think I don't like her anymore . . . maybe."

"That must be a difficult thought to sit with," I said. "I know you've been friends for a long time. You've shared what you're thinking after seeing her, but can you think of an emotion you're feeling?"

"I *feel* . . . sometimes . . . envious." She sank deeper into her chair, as if trying to disappear. "I'm such a bad friend; you're not supposed to be envious of your friends!"

"Your feelings never make you a bad person. There are no good or bad emotions, and being aware of them will help you find more helpful ways to feel."

What Sarah was doing is common for people who are stuck in comparison: they judge themselves for having the emotional habits that comparison brings up. To cope with these negative feelings, we either turn against others or we turn against ourselves. Sarah had turned against her friend initially, then turned against herself for feeling that way. This is one of the most harmful effects of comparison as motivation: it can cause serious damage to our relationships with others and to ourselves, sometimes both at once.

Comparison and Toxic Productivity

Comparison is often used to motivate us to perform better and achieve more. It may start with parents and other authority figures comparing us to siblings, classmates, or other kids in general to point out where they want to see our behavior or performance improve. But comparison can just as easily come from within ourselves. If, like Sarah, we find ourselves getting passed over for opportunities (at work, dating, etc.) or simply admire someone else's talent or confidence in areas where we lack it, it's perfectly natural to envision ourselves in others' shoes.

In the most simple way, we see a straightforward (but not often true) cause and effect: if we are like them, we will get what they have.

But just like shame and perfectionism, this form of motivation is harmful rather than helpful. It compromises our well-being by focusing our thoughts and energy on external markers of achievement instead of on addressing the unmet emotional needs that cause us to doubt and disenfranchise ourselves. Comparison is possibly the most intuitive catalyst for toxic productivity we've discussed so far—when you compare yourself to other people, it's only intuitive to strive for the milestones those people have already reached. From there, it's a slippery slope into unhealthy habits of overworking, avoidance, and burnout.

In comparing ourselves to others, we're not only borrowing goals and aspirations from other people's lives instead of reaching for the ones that are authentically meaningful to us; we're also borrowing their "playbook" for achieving those goals. Recall from chapter 2 that when we chase productivity that does not align with our own values, we can easily begin to deprioritize things that matter to us. Doing so makes it difficult to stay on track, feel fulfillment and an internal sense of purpose, and also be authentic with those around us and ourselves. Rather than showing up as ourselves, we subconsciously try to show up as someone else. Inauthenticity heightens feelings of anxiety, stress, and overwhelm while stoking envy, insecurity, and the flagship issue of the millennial generation, the fear of missing out (FOMO).

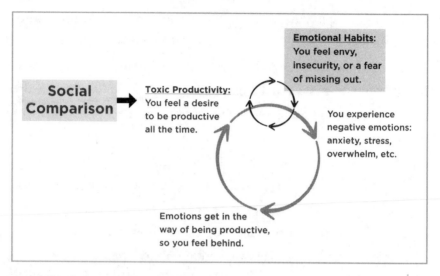

All of these effects were on full display with Jeremy after his partner unexpectedly ended their relationship. In our very first sessions together, Jeremy had repeatedly assured me that (as he saw it) dating is just a numbers game.

"The more people you date," he asserted, "the higher the chance of meeting *The One*."

He came back to this maxim again and again whenever I suggested that taking a break or even slowing his dating schedule down might ultimately make his search for a partner more (for lack of a better word) productive. He insisted that I was wrong. "I have to be proactive and seize every opportunity. If I'm not actively dating, I might miss out."

But when he returned after his "ghosting," Jeremy seemed far less self-assured than before. Our sessions were now filled with him making negative comments about himself, undermining his abilities, and second-guessing himself.

"Sometimes I wonder if I can even be in a relationship anymore," he mumbled. "I've been single for so long. I'm sure it shows when I meet someone." It was uncharacteristic of Jeremy to let himself be sad in front of me, instead of hiding behind practicality or trying to be smarter than the therapist. He shared these vulnerable thoughts with such ease that I wondered how many times he had had this conversation with himself before.

"Tell me more," I urged.

"Some of my other single friends are just so easygoing with girls," he mused. "I get all bungled up and get in my head. Sometimes I feel like I ramble a lot." He sat back in defeat. "It shouldn't be *this* hard, you know? So many of my friends literally met their husbands and wives randomly on the street, or on Hinge, and they just got into a relationship. It was so easy for them—I can't figure out what I'm not doing that they did."

Comparison was doing two things to Jeremy: (1) It was making him question his worthiness because he didn't match his expectations, which were based on what other people were doing; and (2) the more he questioned himself, the more he pushed himself toward a relationship. What Jeremy needed to do was determine whether he wanted a partner because of his own values or because it was something he "should" do. My suspicion was that it was the latter, which meant he wasn't living a life aligned with his values. Perhaps, despite his completed checklist of qualifications, he wasn't actually ready for a relationship.

A few sessions later, I asked him what would happen if he met someone who wasn't the best fit for him but was interested in having a relationship with him. I was trying to get him to see if he valued being in a relationship or having a relationship status.

"Where does romance or compatibility fit into this?" I asked.

"You can build romance, can't you?" he countered. "And compatibility . . . I mean, I can change, she can change. At this stage in my life I think being in a relationship, even if it's not a perfect fit, is better than being alone."

I ventured to ask the question no single person wants to hear: "What's so bad about being alone?"

"What will people think? It'll mean there's something wrong with me. If I can't find a partner, I must be a loser."

"But what value do *you* think a relationship will bring to *your* life?" It was a question I'd asked many times—I wondered if emphasizing certain words might help it land for him. "How will a partner fit into what *you* want for *yourself*?"

"I want the same things everyone wants." Jeremy ticked them off on his fingers. "A place to live, a good job, money, and a partner. I mean, that's what my parents have, that's what my grandparents had, it's what everyone works toward."

While Jeremy still couldn't answer the question I was asking him, he had revealed an important point in his thinking: he was keenly aware of what others (his parents and grandparents in particular) wanted for him, but he was still not very aware of what he wanted for himself. Prioritizing the expectations he perceived of his family, culture, and community naturally made him overly concerned with how others viewed him, fostering self-critical judgments rather than connection to his own needs and values. Until Jeremy could focus on his true values regarding a relationship—what he wanted in a partner and why he wanted to be someone else's partner—he would continue showing up for dates in a transactional, checklist-oriented mindset that would likely end any potential relationship before it could begin.

Exercise

Finding Your Comparing Style

It's important to know the signs of the comparing mind. Being more aware of these will give insight into how you view productivity, including whether you are internalizing or externalizing. Reflect on your comparing habits with the following questions:

- How does comparing yourself to others show up for you?
- What are the patterns you engage in when you are stuck in the *comparing mind*?
- How do you feel right after you have comparison-based thoughts, both in your body and your emotions?

Signs You're in the Comparing Mind

There are a few hallmark signs of the comparing mind. Many of these are difficult to identify as being problematic because we do them so often; we grow up around these types of messages and we rarely stop to question whether they are helpful or harmful.

Below is a list of common thought patterns that we can get stuck in when we are in the comparing mind. As you read through it, consider whether you recognize any of them in yourself:

- You are hyper-critical of yourself and minimize your successes. You might think, for example, "Oh, it's not such a big deal that I got a good review, it's not like I got promoted like Nina did."
- You rush from one milestone, idea, or goal to the next because you "feel behind." You might think, "I must get a PhD. We don't need to celebrate my master's degree—it's just a stepping stone."

- You feel jealous of others and judge them harshly. You might think, for example, "Adam just got lucky—everything comes so easily for him."

- You decline opportunities because they don't feel as big or important as someone else's. You might think, "I'm not wasting my time by doing that interview; it's not for a big publication like Serena had last month."

- You make decisions wanting to emulate another person's decisions or lifestyle without being intentional about your own decisions. You might think, "All our friends are moving out of the city and into homes in the suburbs—it's about time for us to buy a house too."

The Emotional Habits
of the Comparing Mind

We seldom have conscious awareness of how intensely we are comparing ourselves to others. We may only realize it much later, or it's possible we don't notice we're doing it at all. Few of us scroll through social media consciously thinking *Hmm, I wonder how I measure up against other people.* Comparison is a lot sneakier than that, and the unhealthy emotional habits it breeds—envy, insecurity, and FOMO— just seem like mundane aspects of life in our world today.

I remember when I was caught up in unhealthy emotional habits after a romantic relationship from my early twenties ended because of infidelity. In the months that followed, I was unconsciously comparing myself to anyone who looked like the other girl. It came to a point where I would freeze on the bus or subway, on the street, or on my way to class if I saw anyone who reminded me of the other girl. I would feel a blinding rush of intense heat swelling up in my chest; my mind would cloud over with paralyzing negative self-talk, leaving me feeling small, ashamed, and unworthy.

If you asked me back then, I wouldn't have been able to pinpoint that I was comparing myself to other girls as a way of coping with a deeper, more painful sense of insecurity. I thought I was just dealing with heartbreak, that this constant comparison was normal. In the same way, it's easy to believe that emotions of jealousy and FOMO are simply endemic to our generation's culture and lifestyle. Being surrounded at all hours of the day by stories and images of people living their "best life" and inundated by a vast and diverse array of opportunities for entertainment and optimization, jealousy and FOMO are like light pollution or heavy traffic—just part of the cost of living in a modern urban landscape.

The bigger issue underlying these emotions—*inauthenticity*—dulls our ability to identify these emotions for what they are, not to mention our awareness of their very real impact. Sarah's comment about her friend, Yasmin—"I think I don't like her anymore"—turned out to be only the tip of the iceberg. As we continued to explore that emotion, she explained that every time she saw this friend, she became hyper-aware of the friend's minor flaws or faults. Sometimes, Sarah admitted, she even found herself looking for petty ways to judge her friend. Her jealousy functioned like a defense mechanism, trying its best to even the playing field between herself and this friend (*Yasmin might own her own apartment, but at least I don't snort when I laugh*) while at the same time isolating Sarah from what used to be a genuine, nourishing connection.

Meanwhile Jeremy's FOMO-driven approach to dating was having a very material impact on his life. After hearing him mention in a session that he felt bored, I said, "I don't hear you talk much about the things you love doing. Roughly how much time do you spend on doing things you love?"

"I know what you're trying to do," he laughed. "You're trying to show me that I'm not spending enough time on hobbies and self-care. But I've intentionally put aside my personal interests for now. The reality is that I can't pursue a relationship and spend time and money on activities for myself."

I was taken aback—I hadn't asked him anything about money. "Out of curiosity, how much do you spend each month on dating?"

Jeremy spent a few minutes tallying up restaurant bills, bar tabs, tickets to movies, concerts, and other activities, and of course the costs of taxis or Ubers before, during, and after each date, not to mention the premium subscription cost for each of the dating platforms he used. The amount was staggering. The look on his face suggested this was the first time he'd done this calculation.

All these instances serve as proof of the old adage "comparison is the thief of joy." And as we've learned, motivation without joy is ultimately unsustainable. It not only undermines our ability to show up as our best and truest selves, but if we ever reach our goal, it may not even prove authentically satisfying.

Transforming the Comparing Mind to the Inspired Mind

Social comparison is a learned behavior, which means we can unlearn it. However, it is also possible to repurpose comparison into something that can benefit you. Comparisons can help you see other people's strengths, learn from their mistakes, and show you who you might be compatible with (whether romantically or platonically). For example, comparing yourself to a coworker might give you important information about their style of working versus your style of working, which can give you good insight on whether you will work well together.

On an even deeper level, author and psychiatrist Ravi Chandra writes in his book *Facebuddha: Transcendence in the Age of Social Networks* that comparison can be an entry point into inner reflection by asking yourself what the comparison is telling you about yourself, what you want, and how you want to live.[42] This is what I call cultivating the *inspired mind*.

Shifting from the comparing mind to the inspired mind starts with noticing where you direct your attention. In the comparing mind, the focus is on the other person: what they're doing, how they're living, and what their choices look like. In contrast, the inspired mind keeps the focus on you; instead of "Why don't I have what they have?", it asks you to consider "What is this telling me about myself?"

Sarah is the perfect example of how the comparing mind can be transformed into the inspired mind. When we started working together, Sarah's goals were defined by other people's lives. Listening to her share anecdotes and encounters with her friends, it was clear that there was a misalignment between what she wanted, what she thought she wanted, and what she had. But she spent so much of her spare time focusing on what her friends had and how she could follow their path that she wasn't able to focus on what she had the power to change or work toward in her own life.

To help her discover her authentic goals, I asked her to pause the reflections on her friends and instead consider what she thought about herself. This was initially difficult for her to do—many of her responses were things other people had told her or ways she thought she ought to be. When I pointed this out, she was silent for a moment, then began to cry.

"You know what I think most often about myself? I wonder, *What's wrong with me? Why are things so hard for me?*"

Seeing how painful this reflection was for her, I tried to lead her more gently through it. "Let's summarize your experience: you see something about your friend's life on social media, and it activates a series of thoughts in your mind—*Her life is easy. She gets everything she wants. Why are things so hard for me? What am I doing wrong?* These thoughts make you feel overwhelmed and sad, and you shut down." I looked at her for confirmation and she nodded, tears still welling up in her eyes. "Staying in this mindset for a minute, let's explore this question: What emotional experience do I feel like I'm missing, and how can I connect to that?"

I explained to Sarah that this thought exercise wasn't about setting another goal or adding one more thing to her checklist. Rather, it was about finding her intention for the goals she set and the things she pursued. Where goals are discrete objectives we want to achieve in different parts of our life, an intention is what we want to feel from those achievements, the emotional experience that binds together the larger narrative of our life. Reframing our moments of envy, insecurity, and FOMO from goals to intentions is how we transform the comparing mind into the inspired mind.

Let's look at another example. Imagine that you and your partner are out to dinner with another couple. You and your partner get into an argument on the way there and sit side by side in tight silence, perhaps keeping a thin line of separation between your bodies. The other couple, in contrast, are laughing with each other, rubbing shoulders, holding hands, and sharing bites of food from their plates. On the way home, you begin to compare your relationship to theirs: *Our friends have a better relationship than us. They're always laughing and never fight.*

You could stay with the comparing mind and ruminate on everything you and your partner do wrong in comparison to the other couple. Alternatively, you could tap into the inspired mind and reframe this negative thought as an opportunity for finding your intention: *They seem to be really connected and close. I want a deeper connection between my partner and me.*

Now you have something to work toward! With "deeper connection" as your intention, you can have a heartfelt (and productive!) conversation with your partner, one that doesn't incite negative feelings of comparison with your friends but rather explores ways that you can work together to achieve something that is authentically meaningful to both of you.

Exercise

Transforming your Comparing Mind to an Inspired Mind

To understand this transformation process better, let's look again at the thoughts listed at the beginning of this chapter and see how we can reframe them:

- Original thought: *Her life is going so well. How am I so behind?*

- Mindset shift: *I accept where my life is, but where can I make changes to achieve the life I want?*

  ———

- Original thought: *Their relationship seems so perfect; all we do is fight.*

- Mindset shift: *There are unique, great things about my relationship as well as some difficult conversations we need to have.*

  ———

- Original thought: *His house is always so damn clean. I can't even keep the sink free of dishes.*
- Mindset shift: *I am doing what is possible for me, and I can learn some organizing tips from him.*

———

- Original thought: *Everyone else I know has a master's degree; I'll never be as good as them.*
- Mindset shift: *My worth is not connected to my education and my experience matters, no matter what.*

Take a moment to think about a few of your most common comparison statements or thoughts. If you'd like, you can write them down on a sheet of paper. Using the examples above as a guideline, can you transform them into an Inspired Mind statement or thought?

You Have to Trust the Fall

After working together for almost six months, Sarah came into my office, excited to share something that had happened with me.

"I went bouldering over the weekend with my friend, Victoria. As we were both making our way up, there were times she was ahead of me, and times I was ahead of her. Both of us also were taking totally different routes and grabbing on to different rocks to pull ourselves up. As I was making my way up, I had a thought, and I haven't been able to stop thinking about it since: *There are many different ways to get to the top, but the only way to actually get to the top was to take one step at a time and to trust the fall.*" She paused, her eyes bright and her face smiling. I let the pause hang in the air, wanting her to savor this moment of growth and joy for herself.

"That sounds so insightful. What about this thought has stayed with you?"

"I've spent so much time and energy this year thinking about what other people are doing," she said, "that I stopped focusing on what I'm doing . . . or not doing. I'm not pulling myself up or looking ahead to the next rock to grab on to; I'm just watching my friends. I realized that doing that was making me feel like I was on the sidelines of my own life, waiting for it to begin." She stopped and leaned back, her eyes filling with tears, before continuing. "But my life isn't going to magically start someday—I'm in it right *now*. I can either live it or stay stuck in the same place."

This was a powerful moment for Sarah: deciding to be an active participant in her life. Using the insights she gained from examining her comparison-based thoughts, Sarah would be able to find a new path forward for herself. The road to releasing herself from the confines of the comparing mind was a long one, but I was extremely proud of her for taking the first steps.

Key Takeaways

- Comparing ourselves to others is a common experience. This is known as the comparing mind, which is focused on what other people have and what we do not have.

- Comparison acts like a catalyst for toxic productivity; by comparing your life to other people's lives, you push yourself to meet their milestones as well, even if they do not match up to your values.

- The comparison mindset can show up in your emotional habits, such as developing impostor syndrome, feeling insecure, or making fear-based decisions, and having resentment toward others.

- When we compare ourselves to others, we can turn against people in our life, which impacts our relationships negatively, or we can turn against ourselves, which impacts our self-esteem and self-worth.

- The opposite of the comparison mindset is the inspired mind: using what others have as inspiration to help you move closer to your goals. The comparison mindset is focused on others; the inspired mindset is focused on you.

Chapter 8

Quiet Your Inner Critic

"Things which matter most must never be
at the mercy of things which matter least."

—Johann Wolfgang von Goethe

You know those moments where you feel really seen? When someone says something that you've always felt to be deeply true, but you always thought you were the only one who felt this way? This happened to me when I was listening to one of my favorite podcasts, *How to Be a Better Human*. The guest, Stanford psychologist Meag-gan Ann O'Reilly, offered this insight: "When you say 'should,' you're already behind."[43]

I was blown away by how concisely she had put my experience into words. She was referring to the power of the inner critic, the negative self-talk based on "I should" thoughts. I struggle with the pressure of "I should" thoughts from time to time, as well. (Therapists are human, after all.) I remember when I was trying to build a habit of waking up early to get a little writing done before work. I would sometimes miss the alarm and end up sleeping an extra 10 to 15 minutes. Not the end of the world, right? Wrong. The moment I looked at my phone to check the time, the thought that popped into my head was *Ugh— I've wasted time already; this day is going to be crap*. With my mind already occupied by negative thoughts before I had even left my bed, it was only natural that those thoughts affected how well I wrote that morning, or if I wrote at all. In my mind, I had already lost, and the "should" turned into a self-defeating prophecy.

What Is an Inner Critic?

Our mental world is largely made up of us speaking to ourselves about ourselves. When the self-talk is positive and uplifting, it can help boost our self-worth and emotional resilience. However, when the self-talk is negative and critical, it can diminish our mood, self-worth, and sense of competence. In short, it becomes an adversary to healthy productivity, and instead encourages toxic productivity.

Most of the time, self-talk happens spontaneously; the thoughts almost feel automatic. Rarely do we stop to consider the nature and quality of these thoughts. Consider the following questions to see how you speak to yourself:

- What would be your first thought when you open your eyes after snoozing your alarm or waking up late?

- What thought might you have when you accidentally spill coffee on yourself?

- What thought might you have about yourself if you forgot a friend's birthday?

- How would you talk to yourself if you don't do well at a presentation at work?

As far as we know, the power of self-reflection or introspection is uniquely human. We are the only animals on this planet that can think about ourselves or refer to ourselves in our minds. The human brain developed the capacity for self-talk so we could reflect on both the past and the future to ensure our safety and survival.[44] Self-talk still serves that same purpose, helping us make meaning from the things we are experiencing and better understand ourselves and others.

The ability to talk ourselves through things begins in early childhood. If you watch young children play on their own, you'll notice that they often narrate their actions or speak out loud the instructions they've been given. In developmental and educational psychology, this is known as *scaffolding* because it creates a structure of support for our thoughts.[45] As we grow older, this external dialogue becomes internal. We start developing an inner voice that either cheers us on or tears us down.

Since you are with your thoughts 100 percent of the time, the quality of your thoughts really matters, even the ones that happen spontaneously and outside of conscious awareness.[46] When self-talk is negative—that is, its tone and language are critical, harsh, or punitive rather than constructive or reflective—we call it an *inner critic*. The way you think about and talk to yourself guides what you expect from yourself and what you give yourself permission to do.

By casting doubt on your capabilities, the inner critic activates the toxic productivity mindset.

The Inner Critic and Toxic Productivity

The inner critic and toxic productivity are deeply intertwined. This is because our thoughts influence everything that fuels the toxic mindset, all the dynamics we've explored in the previous chapters: low self-worth, shame, comparison, and perfectionism, as well as the unhealthy emotional habits of envy, FOMO, impostor syndrome, and insecurity. The emotional overwhelm created by the inner critic leads you right into avoidance behaviors that also fuel the toxic cycle. It's like a set of dominos: one falls and the rest follow suit, one by one.

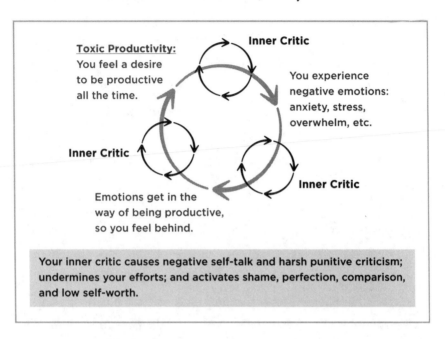

Toxic Productivity: You feel a desire to be productive all the time.

Inner Critic

You experience negative emotions: anxiety, stress, overwhelm, etc.

Inner Critic

Inner Critic

Emotions get in the way of being productive, so you feel behind.

Your inner critic causes negative self-talk and harsh punitive criticism; undermines your efforts; and activates shame, perfection, comparison, and low self-worth.

Let's examine how this can play out in real life.

From the moment I met Lara, she looked like the picture of an ambitious, focused, successful woman. But the longer I worked with her, the more I noticed that she tended to open each of our sessions with an anecdote from the previous week which concluded in an inner critic thought, such as:

- "I should be doing more for my kids; they deserve better."

- "Why can't I be as organized at work as I used to be? I was so on top of things."

- "I'm always so busy, but nothing I do seems to be enough."

- "I bet other moms handle this way better than I do."

- "Nobody understands how much pressure I put on myself to meet everyone's expectations."

I pointed my observation out to her one day. "Has it ever struck you that even with your partner telling you that you're doing too much, you seem to always feel like you're not doing enough?"

She blinked. "I mean, he just says that because he wants me to spend more time with him. He doesn't actually know anything about what I'm doing."

"Are you sure?" I pushed back. "He knows what your job involves. He knows where you are when you're not at home. And I'm sure you tell him the reasons behind having to work late or go into the office on the weekends."

"Right . . ." She waved her hands impatiently. "I just mean that he doesn't know whether I'm doing enough or not. He's not my boss."

"I'm going to challenge you on that, so bear with me." I smiled as I continued. "Because whenever you win a case or get a promotion, or a raise, or an award for your company, he can reasonably conclude that you must be doing enough. I think most people would draw that conclusion. I'm curious why *you* don't see that."

Lara paused, her mouth half open as if to speak. But no words came out.

"Who is telling you that you're not doing enough at work?" I asked. "Or take the example of your kids—you say they deserve better, that you should be doing more for them. But have they said anything like that to you?"

I watched Lara as she thought intently for a moment.

"No one's told me that," she finally responded. "I just . . . I know there's so much more I could be doing. Or I see where I left something not as well done as it could have been. Maybe nobody else sees it, but I see it. I know how I could have done better."

It was clear that, appearances to the contrary, Lara was exhausted and emotionally overwhelmed. She could list off her accomplishments to anyone who asked, but in the privacy of her own mind, she was not able to feel confident in her strengths or acknowledge her wins. Despite how much pride she took in getting everything done perfectly, she couldn't shut off the voice of her negative self-talk. The only way she knew to combat that voice was to strive for the next level of success and hope that was enough to satisfy her inner critic. What Lara didn't realize was that this was the one area where she could never excel, no matter how much she did or how well she performed. This is because the inner critic doesn't deal with facts. Its currency is fear.

Identifying Your Inner Critic

If we don't build awareness of where our thoughts come from and how they make us feel, we don't feel compelled to question what they say; we just accept them as the truth. That's the biggest leverage our inner critic has—it makes us believe the negative self-talk in our mind is fact instead of thoughts subject to passing emotions, biases, and interpretation. Lara had no idea that her thoughts might be coming from somewhere other than her observation of her own performance. It's no wonder she struggled with perfectionism (and with accepting her partner's feedback)—the constant stream of negative self-talk from her inner critic made it impossible for her to feel a sense of accomplishment, no matter how much she got done.

Most of us assume that our inner voice is our own. In fact, our thoughts tend to be a combination of many different influences in our lives: family, friends, the culture in which we were brought up, the culture we inhabit today, society at large, education, and many more. It's like one big group discussion taking place at all times in the back of our minds, with certain voices coming in louder depending on the situation we are in.

A lot of times, people forget that they have the option to reject their thoughts. Of course, we pick and choose which thoughts to accept and which to reject all the time—we just might not do it consciously. Lara was very skilled at rejecting thoughts introduced by her partner, such as *Maybe I could use a day to sleep in* or *Maybe the kids would be fine with one after-school activity instead of three.* Meanwhile, she persisted in believing the thoughts that said she wasn't doing enough, despite the overabundance of evidence that she was great at her job.

We've already discussed how the brain favors the familiar (because familiar feels safe) and when it encounters something unfamiliar, it leans toward a negative interpretation (because caution feels safer than optimism). The same is true for how we unconsciously select which thoughts to accept and which ones to reject. So rather than examining your thoughts in and of themselves, a more effective approach is to question where they come from. In other words, does the voice of your inner critic sound like anyone you recognize? Even if you don't literally "hear" it, does it use language that you recognize from a certain context? Does it use certain words (like *should*) over and over again, or come back to the same topics, such as a difficult experience you've had or an idea that someone taught you? Does it have a general attitude toward the world—cynical, anxious, or condescending—that you associate with anyone in particular?

Don't be surprised if you get an answer you didn't expect. When I examined the voice of my inner critic, I was surprised to find that it did not belong to any real person in my life, past or present. Instead, it was an amalgamation of every expectation I had of who I "should" be. It was a shock to realize that I was being guided through the lens of someone who doesn't even exist, not through the lens of who I really am. From that point on, whenever my negative self-talk came up, I'd pause and ask myself, *Who is really saying this?* This helped me differentiate between thoughts that were authentically my own and thoughts being offered by my inner critic. Knowing who is behind the voice of your inner critic offers you a way to filter the thoughts it brings up. Is the person this voice comes from reliable? In my case, the answer was no—that person didn't even exist. Is this the voice of someone whom you admire or respect? Is it even someone you trust to have your best interest at heart? If the answer is no, that's probably a good reason to question that voice more closely before following it.

Exercise

Who Is Your Inner Critic?

Are you curious about where your inner critic comes from? Does your negative self-talk remind you of one or more person(s) from your life from the past, or perhaps even the present? Is this the voice of a real person or someone you imagine? Use the following prompts to reflect on your inner critic:

- My inner critic reminds me of . . .
- This is because . . .
- My first memory of this thought is from . . .

Using Critical Thinking with Your Inner Critic

Once you've identified the voice of your inner critic, you can intelligently question what it is saying. This is something I often practiced with Julia, who was having a hard time updating her résumé because it made her anxious. One of the things she struggled with the most was trusting herself enough to know when the inner critic was telling the truth or when it was acting from a place of harsh judgment.

"Let's think about this," I suggested. "If you ignored your inner critic, what could or would happen?"

"I don't know. I mean, it's not all wrong, all the time." It seemed she was thinking out loud to herself more than answering my question.

Julia was right. While you don't want to reflexively believe everything your inner voice says, it does have a benefit: to protect you from pain. Your inner critic comes from the part of the brain that is always scanning your environment for the potential of rejection, humiliation, abandonment, or emotional distress; it uses criticism and judgment to keep you far away from anything that could bring you pain.

Your inner critic is not acting to shame you or bring you down; it's acting to protect. The problem is that your inner critic will take this protective role as far as it can. It will gladly keep you far away from excitement or opportunities to grow if it suspects there could be any possibility of pain. This is what Julia's inner critic was doing to her. Every time she began to write her own qualifications on her résumé, her inner critic whispered, *What happens if they hire you and then find out you're not an expert at this?* Or *This position is way out of your league. You'll never even get an interview—they'll just look at this résumé and laugh.*

Julia needed to build a *reality filter*, a mindset that uses a gentle, open-ended exploration of what the inner critic is saying. Instead of accepting the inner critic's message at face value, a strong reality filter uses critical thinking to deconstruct its judgments with two important questions:

1. What is the evidence that you're right?

2. What becomes possible if you are wrong?

Answering these questions will reveal the whole picture that the inner critic can only see one side of. By showing you the potential benefit of believing the opposite, this strategy helps expand your thought process to include different perspectives and possibilities your inner critic would never have dreamed of.

Profiling Your Inner Critic

You can also loosen the grip of your inner critic by getting to know its style or type. You'll find several of the inner critic's typical styles in the following list. As you read through them, reflect on which type(s) of inner critic you believe you have:

- **The Blamer:** Makes everything your fault (*You are not as good as others because you don't work hard enough.*)

- **The Polarizer:** Looks at things in black-and-white terms—either purely good/productive or purely bad/unproductive (*You are lazy for sleeping in.*)

- **The Magnifier:** Is hyper-focused on negative things that have happened while filtering out the positive (*You haven't accomplished anything!*)

- **The Person In-Crisis:** Is hyper-focused on possible negative outcomes, convinced that the worst-case scenario is going to happen (*Everyone will move forward in life, but you'll get left behind.*)

- **The Realist:** Uses logic and analysis to convince you that you are not enough, not ready, or that things won't work out (*It doesn't make sense for you to try this—just stick to what you know.*)

Using this awareness, you can create an actual character for your inner critic; this supports you in seeing it as separate from you, making it even easier to distinguish its voice from your own authentic thoughts. It also makes it easier to catch your inner critic and cross-examine it with your two key answers—the evidence that it's right and the possibilities if it's wrong—before deciding what to do.

Exercise

Creating a Character Summary of Your Inner Critic

In this exercise, you will create a character summary of your inner critic. When I do this exercise with clients, some come with a list of attributes and personality characteristics, while others make drawings using shapes, color, and style to indicate personality traits of the inner critic. Some create actual characters with names and backstories. The most creative one I've seen was a PowerPoint presentation of the inner critic!

This summary will empower you to analyze whether your inner critic's criticism is helpful or if it is a message you can dismiss. Remember that while the inner critic won't ever go away, you have the power to turn down the volume on what it's saying. Use the following steps to help you get to know your inner critic:

- Take a few moments to reflect on the negative or critical self-talk happening in your head on an average day. How do you talk to yourself when something is not going the way you wanted or if you make a mistake?

- Next, notice the type of your self-talk, using the options in the list in the previous section. Reflect on where you learned to talk or think about yourself like this.

- Earlier in the chapter you reflected on who your inner critic reminds you of. Add that information here. Does the inner critic remind you of someone in your life—maybe a parent or a teacher from the past? Describe the voice and the character around it.

- Give the inner voice a persona:
  - What type of person is your inner critic? How would you describe its personality to someone else?
  - What are its values? What are its perspectives or worldview?
  - What is your inner critic most afraid of?

- Name your inner critic. Giving your negative self-talk a separate identity is a powerful way to differentiate yourself from your inner critic, making it easier to manage, question, or dismiss what it is saying.

- Last, get to know its patterns. When does the inner critic show up? Who does it show up around? What triggers self-criticism or anger toward yourself? Are there specific situations or people it shows up around more often?

- An additional step, if you're up for it, is to get curious about what the inner critic is trying to tell you. Is there often a central message or theme? Ask questions to figure out what the message behind the criticism is—what is it trying to protect you from?

Stop Your Inner Critic from Taking Over

Though the inner critic will likely not disappear completely, you can manage its appearances by making small habit and thought changes that make it less persuasive. As you read through the next sections, think about how you can use the persona you built in the previous section to help make this easier.

Stop Judging Yourself

Judging yourself can become second nature, especially in moments of stress or uncertainty. You might even be unaware of how you are judging yourself. To strengthen your resistance to the influence of the inner critic, it's important to catch those judgmental thoughts in the moment, replacing them with thoughts that encourage your autonomy and resilience. Review the following table, noticing which types of judgments come up most often for you, and then use the righthand column for strategies to shift your mindset.

Judgment	Mindset Shift
You overgeneralize traits about yourself.	Instead, give yourself permission to be complex and changing.
You believe everything you think about yourself.	Instead, ask yourself where you learned these negative interpretations and consider how you can transform them into something more accurate.
You internalize blame for other people's behavior or moods.	Instead, consider what you are directly accountable for, and let the rest be the other person's responsibility.
You avoid discomfort in your life.	Instead, become curious about why things make you uncomfortable, and consider what you might gain if you were willing to endure a little discomfort.

Stop "Should-ing" on Yourself

As we discussed in the opening of this chapter, "I should" statements are self-defeating; they imply that you're already on the losing side. Moreover, they usually ignore any context or progress in your situation. They are rigid rules that you feel you need to follow, based on one of two things: what you were taught (*I should always be nice, no matter what*) and what you see others doing (*All my friends are married, so I should be married*). "I should" statements often refer to your unwanted identity. For example, "I should have had an impeccable presentation" is based on an unwanted identity of being unskilled, unlucky, or less likely to succeed.

It's true that certain "I should" statements are valid, such as, you should recycle, you should eat a balanced diet, you should treat others with respect. So how do we discern when "should" is true and when it is just guilt? The key lies in the nature of the feelings that follow your "I should" thought. Is the thought supporting you or bringing you down? The way in which you treat yourself *in light* of the "I should" determines whether the statement will empower you to be productive in a healthy way or dig you deeper into the toxic productivity mindset.

Like thoughts from the comparing mind, you can reframe "I should" thoughts into genuine, healthy motivation by focusing on the benefit you desire rather than the obligation you feel. When you find yourself thinking "I should" (or "I should not"), rephrase it as "I want" or "I'd like to." For example, instead of "I should have woken up earlier (but I didn't because I'm lazy)," try "I'd like to wake up earlier so I can enjoy my coffee and a few minutes of quiet before the workday begins." You'll be shocked at how much more motivating this feels!

Practice the Pause

Breaking the influence of the inner critic doesn't always come easily. While it might feel satisfying and even thrilling to defy the inner critic in some situations, there can also be times when our inner critic strikes back at our defiance by activating unpleasant reactions or distressing emotions that amplify our negative thoughts. This makes it easy to engage in an argument with those negative thoughts, something the inner critic is perfectly fine with. As long as we don't do whatever it's trying to protect us from, the inner critic will happily keep us arguing all night long. (It may even convince us that the mental exhaustion we feel is proof that we've had a "productive" bout of deep thinking.)

You can cut this tail-chasing exercise short by creating distance between yourself and your inner critic. How can that be possible if these thoughts are coming from inside you? By *engaging your body*, you can create distance between you and your thoughts.

The following exercises will help you to create space when you're struggling with your inner critic:

- **Breathe:** Take three deep breaths—inhale, hold, then slowly exhale. This will slow down your body by increasing the oxygen level in your blood and slowing down your heart rate, giving you time to find mental clarity.

- **Acknowledge the feeling or the thought:** Simply allow yourself, without judgment, to notice your emotions or take in your thought.

- **Change the temperature of your body:** Splash cold water on your face, take a cold shower, or place an ice cube on your wrist or at the base of your neck. This will break the "paralysis" effect of overthinking, allowing you to literally reset your body and mind so that you can approach the issue with a fresh perspective.

Now that we've gone through the process of identifying the inner critic and strategies to curb its influence, let's turn to a concept I love: the inner coach.

Meet Your Inner Coach

When the inner critic shows up, it always helps to have someone in your corner—a friend, family member, or partner who will counteract its negative influence with positive feedback and encouragement. Sometimes, though, you're the one who must be in your own corner. This is the inner coach mindset.

As mentioned before, your inner critic is not your adversary; even when its voice is unhelpful, it is only trying to keep you safe. For that reason, the goal is not to silence your inner critic, but to transform it to something supportive. Where the inner critic increases stress and leads to procrastination, the inner coach promotes progress and celebrates successes, no matter how small. Where the inner critic promotes fear, self-judgment, and toxic productivity, the inner coach encourages creative problem-solving, self-acceptance, and replenishing yourself with rest and play. By cultivating an inner coach, you create a supportive and encouraging environment in your mind that helps you think clearly, act confidently, and make progress toward goals that are truly meaningful to you.

I discovered my inner coach at a yoga class I attended one day. Before starting the practice, the instructor asked us to meditate on a question throughout the class: "How different would your life be if your inner dialogue was supportive toward you?"

I remember thinking, *It's too damn early for such a heavy question.* Still, ever the good student, I spent the class talking to myself the way I would to a friend. Every time I struggled with a pose and a distracting thought popped into my mind (*You'd be better if you came more consistently*), I countered it with a supportive thought (*I'm proud of myself for showing up today*). Even though the instructor's question and the class were challenging, I left with a refreshed, grounded feeling that I carried with me for the rest of my day.

We've seen how powerful self-talk is for influencing our choices. Turning the inner critic into an inner coach leverages that power so you can counter negative thoughts, work through difficult emotions, and replace toxic productivity with healthy motivation and balance. With intentional practice, you can make your inner dialogue supportive instead of destructive.

Maya often felt like her emotional needs were not met at work, by her family, or in her romantic relationships, but she couldn't pinpoint why she repeatedly found herself in the same situations. As we started exploring her decision-making process, we found that when she was presented with a situation where she had to make a decision or express an opinion—from small matters like choosing a dinner spot to larger issues like future planning—her inner critic would completely take over:

There's no point in sharing this; they won't listen to you anyway.

You're wrong for feeling this.

You're being too sensitive and overreacting.

Any authentic feelings she had about the situation were invalidated by her inner critic, often before she could even identify what those feelings were. Occasionally, the feelings she had repressed would eventually find their way to the surface; a small conflict would provoke a big explosion from her that alienated or offended others. This only reinforced Maya's feeling that no one cared and that she didn't deserve to be heard. To earn back a feeling of belonging, she resorted to—you guessed it—overcommitting her time and energy. It's no wonder she felt so burned out.

"When you get so down on yourself—that you're not qualified enough, or you're not doing enough—do you ever try to counteract that voice?" I asked. "Do you ever say things in response like 'I'm doing my best' or 'I've worked hard for this and I deserve it?'"

She thought about this for a few minutes. "Isn't it kind of weird to cheer yourself on? Like, isn't it sort of . . . pretentious?" She finished the question in almost a whisper.

I admit I was a bit thrown off. "Can you tell me more about this idea?"

Maya cleared her throat and settled deeper into the couch. "Well, if I am constantly patting myself on the back, won't that make me arrogant? Won't it encourage me to stop trying to be better?"

Ahh, I get it now, I thought. *Another way to say, "I must be mean to myself to feel motivated."*

"I can see why you'd think that," I said, "and being critical of yourself can show you the areas you need to work on. But I wonder how far that can take you before making you feel bad about yourself? Think about it this way: If you are teaching a young child how to write, would you yell at them about their mistakes to get them to learn, or would you explain to them kindly about the mistakes they are making and work with them to learn?"

Maya didn't hesitate. "No, I would never yell at a child if they didn't know how to do something."

"Then why would you yell at yourself for not knowing how to do something?" I asked. "Don't you deserve the same kindness to help yourself grow?"

I led Maya through a journaling exercise where she would imagine the type of person that would speak kindly to the hypothetical child we'd just discussed. What is that person like? How do they speak? What is their outlook? Then, I asked her to imagine that person talking to her. What would they say? How would they say it? By the end of our session, Maya had made her first contact with someone she didn't know existed: her inner coach.

Meeting Your Inner Coach

Set aside about 45 minutes and go to a place where you feel completely relaxed and safe, and where you will be uninterrupted. This can be a specific place in your home, a café, or even a park. Light a candle if you're indoors, listen to music you love, and create an atmosphere of calmness and joy. Use the following steps to create your inner coach:

1. Imagine an ideal version of yourself or a made-up person who has qualities you appreciate and value. Give this person a name. Describe their personality, attitudes, and habits. Where do they live? How do they act toward strangers? How would they react when given criticism or feedback? How do they view mistakes and failures? For fun, you can get even more detailed—think about what their coffee order is, what they like to do in their free time, anything that helps make them more real and present for you.

2. Imagine an interaction with this person and describe it in your mind. Think about how you would feel in the presence of this person, particularly on a bad day. What would they say if you shared the negative self-talk in your head? How would they soothe or validate you? What kind of impact would they have on your emotions?

3. Invite this person into your thoughts whenever your inner critic is activated. This practice might feel uncomfortable or silly for the first few times. That's okay—keep trying it until it feels right. You can play around with it to make it your own. Try writing out your thoughts and writing counter-thoughts in the inner coach's voice or imagine a conversation between your self-talk and the inner coach. One way to do this is by asking yourself, "What would [inner coach's name] say right now?" Over time, this practice will become second nature.

A few weeks after I introduced the concept of the inner coach to Maya, she came in with a PowerPoint presentation (Yes, she was the one!) in which she had filled out the details of this new supportive character. By crafting her ideal version of an inner coach, she was able to reflect on her emotional needs and think about what she needed to hear when she was being mean to herself. This practice allowed her to find real motivation through kindness, compassion, and supportive self-talk.

Key Takeaways

- We spend a lot of our time with our thoughts, and therefore the quality of how we think and what we say to ourselves impacts our perception.

- The inner critic is the internalized voice of your past experiences (parents, teachers, peers, etc.) from childhood that forms the foundation of your negative self-talk.

- Use critical thinking to differentiate between self-talk and reality so that you can have an accurate perspective of what your inner critic tells you.

- To further counter the effects of the inner critic's actions, we have to cultivate an inner coach—a voice that is supportive, encouraging, and kind.

Chapter 9

The Audacity of Abundance

"You often feel tired, not because you've done too much, but because you've done too little of what sparks a light in you."

—Alexander Den Heijer, *Nothing You Don't Already Know*

Imagine there are two people locked in a room with only one window to the outside world. There is nothing to do in the room and no way for them to get out. How do they pass their time? One person focuses on the rising and setting sun, watches how the birds glide across the sky in different patterns depending on the time of day, looks for rainbows on rainy days, and tries to identify constellations to help them fall asleep. This endeavor keeps their mind occupied and engaged; it may even cultivate curiosity and hope about the world. The other person primarily watches the ground that is visible through the window, noticing the dry and caked mud and the litter strewn across it. This person is very uninspired by the dismal monotony of the sludge.

If you asked them about their experience, their answers are bound to differ. While their situation was the same, their experiences were affected by where they focused their attention. This changed their experience of the room without changing the room itself.

You may have read some version of this parable before.* It's a classic illustration of how powerful our mindset can be in influencing our experiences. What you focus your attention on and what you think about affects your perception of reality. The outlooks of these two people can act as metaphors for two different mentalities: the abundance mindset and the scarcity mindset.

The *abundance mindset*, or the frame of mind of the person who looks toward the sky, is the belief that there is enough in the world for you and for others—enough resources, status, achievements, success, and personal development.[47, 48] In this mentality, you look at the world through a lens of possibility in a way that influences your thoughts, feelings, and decisions. Abundance encourages a proactive mindset that looks for possibility, opportunity, and accountability. This belief both comes from and cultivates a sense of security and self-worth. It's also a holistic path to healthy productivity.

On the other hand, the *scarcity mindset*, or the mentality of the person staring at the unchanging mud, is the belief that what you have, or could have, is inadequate to meet your needs or wants.[49] In this mindset, you believe that the resources available to you—time, energy, money, relationships, opportunities—are finite, which naturally creates a sense of urgency and a reactive state of mind. You must act now or risk missing out. If someone else does something that makes progress toward their goal, you need to do the same or better or you might not reach your goal. It's probably obvious that a scarcity mindset is fuel to the fire of toxic productivity. Having a scarcity mindset in relation to productivity might cause you to view rest as a waste of time or take part in the newest self-improvement trend because "everyone else is doing it."

---

* The parable is an expansion of a quote often attributed to the writer and lecturer Dale Carnegie, but that isn't confirmed.

That's what kept me locked in the toxic mindset: the thought that I had to do everything now. And by everything I really mean everything: advance in my career, nurture my creativity, spend time with loved ones, practice self-care, pursue personal development . . . oh, and have fun. Believing the only opportunity I would ever get to do any of this was *right now*, I pushed myself to optimize and utilize every free moment. You can guess what that led to: feeling completely exhausted and disconnected from myself. The most bizarre part? The pressure to do these things was completely imaginary the entire time.

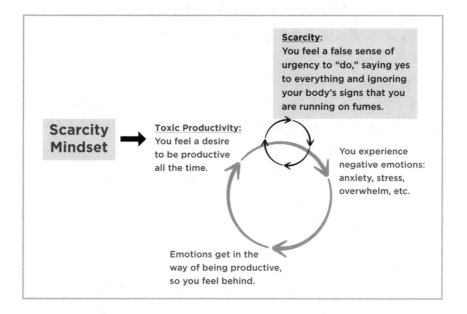

The High Stakes of Scarcity

The scarcity mindset was widely identified by businessman and author Stephen Covey in his 1989 self-help book *The 7 Habits of Highly Effective People*.[50] Covey writes, "Most people are deeply scripted in what I call the Scarcity Mentality. They see life as having only so much, as though there were only one pie out there. And if someone were to get a big piece of the pie, it would mean less for everybody else. *The Scarcity Mentality is the zero-sum paradigm of life*" (emphasis added by me).

What's interesting about the scarcity mindset is that things don't actually have to be scarce for us to experience it. Whether the scarcity is real or imagined, the impact on our thoughts and feelings is the same.[51] This was evident in how Jeremy approached his dating prospects. Statistically, there are more than enough women he could end up in a relationship with; realistically, there is no timeline to finding love. But the pressure Jeremy felt about dating led him to perceive a scarcity of prospects and time. This was impacting his emotions—he was often sad, sometimes felt jealous of his friends, angry at himself, and defeated over the entire situation. It also made him resistant to ideas that could help improve his search for a partner, such as my suggestion that he slow down his search while considering what he really wanted from a relationship and why. This is because scarcity doesn't just have an emotional impact; it has a physical impact on our cognitive ability. It turns out that when we focus on perceived obstacles, limitations, and barriers, we end up with a shortage of mental energy.[52]

In the book *Scarcity*, behavioral scientists Sendhil Mullainathan and Eldar Shafir examine our ability to think when we are under the spell of scarcity.[53] They found that when under a scarcity mindset, the brain's ability to handle and process information is at about the same level as it would be after pulling an all-nighter. We struggle with memory issues, have a hard time concentrating and thinking clearly, and experience emotional instability (being weepy, irritable, etc.) as well as difficulty with critical thinking.

This certainly rings true for me. In the early days of my digital wellness platform, every client relationship felt like it was make-or-break for me. I was thrilled to be offered an opportunity to speak at a conference, but I found myself hesitating to negotiate the speaker fee. I was afraid that if they thought I was too expensive, I would lose the opportunity and wouldn't be able to work with them in the future. After going back and forth on it for a while, I didn't negotiate and instead decided to charge a lower fee. In the weeks that followed, I struggled to craft my presentation; where a higher fee would have allowed me to devote all that time to preparing for the conference, accepting a lower fee meant that I had to work on other projects simultaneously. I couldn't think clearly enough because I was so stressed; despite putting so much effort into the talk, I wasn't happy with my performance or with my compensation. The icing on the cake? I found out later that the other speakers got paid significantly more than me.

Scarcity also creates tunnel vision—you become fixated on what you think you lack (or will lack).[54,55,56] But in looking for an immediate solution to the immediate problem, you can wind up making decisions that are not helpful in the long-term. Jeremy's laser focus on finding a romantic partner meant he had stopped paying as much attention to his friendships. Not only had he practically quit doing things he enjoyed, but he was starting to gain a reputation for being flaky. By making a relationship the cornerstone of his sense of self, he was slowly losing his individuality—his selfhood, if you will—altogether.

How Does Scarcity Show Up for You?

Think about a recent decision you've made—perhaps you made it quickly, without thinking about the consequences. Use the following questions to reflect on how the scarcity mindset shows up for you:

- Think back to when you were making the decision. Were there any fears that showed up? This could be the fear of consequence, the fear of what others might think, or the fear of disappointing someone.

- What message do you think these fears were trying to give you?

- Did you make the decision to alleviate something (anxiety, pressure, etc.) instead of to increase or improve something?

- Do you think you collected all the information needed and fully processed your emotions before making the decision?

- Finally, in what ways did the conditions of scarcity influence your mindset and choices?

Living Under a False Sense of Urgency

Urgency is a symptom of scarcity mindset. As we've learned, when we believe resources (time, opportunity, money, energy, attention, etc.) are limited, every decision seems pressing and every commitment seems necessary. A false sense of urgency also creates what's known as a *psycho-physiological state* of stress that affects us somatically (in our body), cognitively (in our brain), and emotionally.

I can tell you from personal experience how challenging it can be to recognize this sense of urgency as false when you are in the toxic productivity mindset. Looking back to the time I was hurtling toward burnout, I can now see that there were some clear red flags that I was operating under a false sense of urgency. Review the following list and reflect on which ones resonate with you:

- **You experience a dysregulated nervous system:** You feel overstimulated and physically "on edge" more often than not. You might experience tightness in your chest, rapid breathing, or unnecessary sweating. You might have a hard time unwinding or notice that you unconsciously tense your muscles (jaw clenching, curling toes, etc.). These are signs that your stress response is activated. You might have thoughts like *Why am I tired no matter how much I sleep?*

- **You have frantic energy:** You might feel overwhelmed and unsettled, have difficulty focusing, or have racing thoughts. You also might find yourself fidgeting often or feeling like you want to jump out of your skin. You might have thoughts like *I am frazzled.*

- **You feel a desire for immediate action:** You might make quick and impulsive decisions without knowing all the facts, just to get it off your plate or relieve tension. You might have thoughts like *Everything needs to be done now!*

- **You have tunnel vision:** You might be singularly focused on the next step without paying attention to the long-term goal. You might have thoughts like *Nothing else is more important than* _____.

- **Your behavior is self-defeating:** You might engage in emotional regulation through unhealthy defense mechanisms and behavior patterns such as procrastination, distraction, or avoidance. You might often have thoughts like *I can't deal with this right now. I need a blank mind.*

- **You feel an increased sense of responsibility:** You might be operating under the limiting belief that only you can do the things that need to be done, and you may have a hard time delegating and asking for help. You might have thoughts like *Only I can do this, so only I must.*

- **You feel powerless:** You might be feeling like you don't have control over your time or like you are at the mercy of obligations or your calendar. You might have thoughts like *Why are things not happening the way I want?*

Knowing these signs sheds light on scarcity-driven habits and thoughts that you might have normalized. Personally, I thought it was just the norm for me to feel frazzled or tired. Had I recognized these feelings as being a sign of a false belief, I could have been empowered to say no more often. My fear of not having enough (and not being enough) left me with no space to rest, let alone to put my energy into things that gave me a meaningful return. Even if I felt too exhausted to commit to one more thing, my fear of never being asked again compelled me to fit it in.

If you struggle with saying no to things, the following formula has helped me decline a request or invitation when needed, even when I am tempted to overcommit:

- **Thank the person for thinking of you:** Show appreciation that they included you or thought of you for this. It's a nice way to show someone you value their offer. You can say, "Thank you for thinking of me for _____."

- **Ask for time:** In the toxic productivity mindset, saying no activates feelings of shame, FOMO, and guilt. Our impulse is to alleviate this discomfort and act impulsively, to relieve the tension by just saying yes. Instead, create distance between the feeling and the corresponding action you feel compelled to take. One way to do this is to ask for time to respond to the request. Doing so will help alleviate the immediate tension you might feel and give you the opportunity to think about your answer on your own. This will help you make a decision that is right for you. You can say, "Can I get back to you on this?"

- When you're ready to respond, **decline as simply as possible:** You can offer a specific reason, keep it vague, or simply say, "I'm going to have to decline this time." How much information you give is dependent on your relationship with the person asking.

- If you want, **offer an alternative:** This is optional, but it is a good way to let the person know that you care about their situation and are interested in helping them. You can offer them an alternative time you are available or refer them to someone else who might be able to help with the task or attend the event they are asking about. You can say, "I can do (alternative) at (another time)," or "I know (person) who might be able to help you with _____ instead; would you like to connect with them?"

If you struggle under the pressure of a false sense of urgency, before you immediately react or respond, ask yourself whether the situation needs you to take action right now. If this feels too abstract, you can write the answer down to this question: *What might happen if I waited 24 hours to respond?* This reflection will help you differentiate between something that is truly urgent versus something that is only giving the *feeling* of urgency. For instance, if you get the opportunity to give a presentation at a conference that is happening in a few months, there is likely no reason you need to answer the request immediately. You can question your urgency, and you might realize you can wait two days to consider the opportunity before responding.

If you recognize that the situation is not truly urgent, but you still feel mounting pressure or anxiety, focus your attention on self-soothing skills, such as meditation, deep breathing, taking a shower, journaling, or anything that helps you feel more grounded. Learning to tolerate the discomfort of delaying a response is a vital first step in breaking a false sense of urgency.

The Alternative to Scarcity: Abundance

Let's think again about the person in the room who watched the sun, birds, rainbows, and constellations through the window—the abundance mindset. This mindset is grounded in strengths, optimism, and opportunities.[57] We envision the achievements we want to reach, and considering our own skills and self-worth, we are secure in our belief that we can realize them in the future. This doesn't mean we're not grounded in reality; we're simply focused on what is possible instead of what is limited. Those who are more spiritually inclined might call it "manifestation through intention," while the more religiously inclined might call it *gratitude*. Productivity enthusiasts call it a "growth mindset."

We know that our response to scarcity is the same whether the scarcity is real or imagined. This raises an interesting question: If we can think ourselves into an imagined scarcity, then shouldn't the opposite also be true?

What Does Abundance Feel Like?

A scarcity mindset fuels urgency and fear, and it can make us feel on edge or nervous. Let's see instead what an abundance mindset might feel like:

1. Sit in a quiet space and notice your body. Where are you holding tension? Which parts of your body feel stuck? Use one or two words to describe your energy in this moment.

2. Set a timer for two minutes.

3. Close your eyes and take a few deep breaths. Now, imagine your favorite childhood memory, the best vacation you ever took, or being in a place where you feel very safe. Imagine having your favorite person there with you. Imagine that you are doing something that you love, and the weather is exactly the way you like it. Imagine there is a table with your favorite foods and drinks, and your favorite music is playing in the background. Try to be as detailed as possible.

4. When the timer goes off, open your eyes, and notice your body. What is the tension like in your body? What one or two words would you use now to describe your current energy? How is it different from two minutes ago?

If you feel a little more relaxed at the end of this exercise, it's because guided imagery and visualization lower stress and improve mood.[58]

A mindset, at the end of the day, is just a collection of thoughts, beliefs, and opinions. You have the power to choose which mindset to cultivate—scarcity or abundance. That said, you can't just "shift" your way into a different life. There must be follow-up action to implement a mindset shift as a change in your habits. An abundance mindset channeled into your habits is the key to nurturing abundance in your life.

Mindset Shifts to Cultivate Abundance

Openness to Change

The scarcity mindset wants you to stay with what's familiar—when you know something, it feels easier to control. However, limiting ourselves to the same experiences reinforces the belief that there are no other options besides the ones we have already experienced. Having new experiences opens us up to newer possibilities and opportunities, developing the belief that there is more out there for us than we have experienced yet.

The fear-based scarcity mindset focuses on the effort it takes to change while preventing us from seeing the potential benefits it could bring. When confronted with a potential change, you can initiate a mindset shift by asking yourself, "Is there anything about this change I can be excited about?"

Under-scheduling

The scarcity mindset leads to toxic productivity by trying to "make the most" of every free minute. By intentionally under-scheduling, you can keep your stress levels low, making it easier to calm the feeling of overwhelm that encourages a scarcity mindset. If you think something will take 20 minutes, allot 30 minutes for it. If getting somewhere shows 15 minutes on the map, plan to leave with 25 minutes to get there. If you have back-to-back appointments, schedule a 5- to 10-minute buffer in the middle.

Reframe Limiting Beliefs

Limiting beliefs are ideas or perspectives about yourself or the world that can hold you back from doing things that make you happy. It can even cause you to begin questioning your needs or lowering your standards under the notion that something is better than nothing. The result is that you wind up committing yourself and your resources to something that is not aligned with your values or something that doesn't make you happy. It also leads to living in a state of fear: fear of lacking something you need, fear of missing out, or fear of being left behind.

One way to start transforming your scarcity mindset to an abundance mindset is to recognize how your thoughts or habits might be reinforcing the idea of scarcity in your life. Are your own thoughts limiting you from moving forward? What is the evidence that supports your belief; is there any evidence against it?

A habit shift will not happen overnight, but it can grow surprisingly quickly when you practice it in your daily life. Over time, these small habits will shift your mindset without any conscious effort, empowering you to step out of the toxic productivity mindset and develop a healthier relationship with productivity.

Abundance Mindset	Scarcity Mindset
1. Flexible thinking	1. Black-and-white thinking
2. Collaborative	2. Competitive
3. Resources are infinite	3. Resources are finite
4. Leaves you feeling excited	4. Leaves you feeling overwhelmed
5. Curiosity-based thinking	5. Fear-based thinking
6. Takes challenges as opportunities	6. Takes challenges as limitations
7. Big-picture, long-term vision	7. Short-term, goal-based vision

Abundance Is Not the End, But a Means to an End

What would change in your life if you believed things were possible for you? The turning point for me was the story I shared earlier, when I lowballed my speaking fee due to my scarcity mindset. After finding out that I had been paid less than other speakers, I knew I needed to confront myself using reflections, fact-check my beliefs, and learn to tolerate the discomfort of potentially losing an opportunity.

These mindset shifts allowed me to further step away from seeing my opportunities as limited. My scarcity mindset would often say, *You don't have any other choice but to accept what's been given to you, you can only be a speaker because that's what you've always done.* My mindset shifts led me to another thought: *What other choices do I have in this situation?* This led to the biggest change I experienced: I started seeing myself as more than a speaker—I was able to expand my services to paid creative (written, video, and audio) content and courses. When I think of scarcity versus abundance, I often find myself going back to the work of Viktor Frankl, an Austrian psychiatrist and neurologist who survived the Holocaust. Frankl wrote, "Everything can be taken from a man* but one thing: the last of the human freedoms—to choose one's attitude in any given set of circumstances, to choose one's own way."[59]

Frankl went on to spend the remainder of his life helping people remember the power of human choice and find their purpose. His work is a testament to the fact that that we can choose what we pay attention to and that can change the way we perceive our own life.

---

* The term *man* is being used here to denote all of humanity, and not specific to *man* as a gender.

As illustrated by the parable at the beginning of the chapter, how you perceive things and what you focus on creates your reality. On one hand, that's a scary thought because it reminds us that our thoughts have so much power. But on the other hand, it's an empowering thought—if you can influence your thoughts, you can in turn influence your reality.

Exercise

Transforming Scarcity Into Abundance

Let's go back to the experience you chose in the *How Does Scarcity Show Up for You?* exercise. We will use the same information you filled in previously, but this time, we will add a final step to it, transforming the scarcity mindset to one of abundance:

- Think back to when you were making the decision. Were there any fears that showed up? This could be the fear of consequence, the fear of what others might think, or the fear of disappointing someone.

- What message do you think this fear was trying to give you?

- Did you make the decision to alleviate something (anxiety, pressure, etc.) instead of to increase or improve something?

- Do you think you collected all the information needed and fully processed your emotions before making the decision?

- In what ways did the conditions of scarcity influence your mindset and choices?

- In what ways could you think or act differently to develop an abundance mindset in the same situation?

Key Takeaways

- There are two mindsets in which we can look at our time, resources, and opportunities: abundance or scarcity.

- Abundance is the mindset that there is always more: more to learn, more to grow, and more to share. Scarcity is the mindset that there isn't enough: not enough time, not enough resources, and not enough opportunities.

- A scarcity mindset impacts us at a cognitive level, hindering our ability to process information and make thoughtful decisions; it also creates a false sense of urgency to act now.

- An abundance mindset can be cultivated through regulating emotions, reframing limiting beliefs, and allowing room for flexibility in our plans.

Chapter 10

Rest and Rejuvenation

"Spend your free time the way you like,
not the way you think you're supposed to."

**—Susan Cain, *Quiet: The Power of Introverts
in a World that Can't Stop Talking***

When I was moving from Toronto to New York City, I came across an old journal while clearing out my things. It must have been from when I was in my early twenties. One specific entry that caught my eye started off with a bold claim on the top of the page: *In complacency is death*. Scrawled underneath that was another heavy line: *Stagnant waters hold no value*. The remainder of the entry detailed all the ways that I was going to achieve my goals, ending with a pledge to "never stop the movement toward more."

Reading this so many years later, I felt sadness for the younger version of me, whose identity was so infused with productivity. I thought about all the anguish I'd felt over the years, pushing myself toward "success" while feeling like nothing was ever good enough. Looking back, I'm not sure I even knew the meaning of success or what I was pursuing. One thing was clear, though: I held a strong belief that the opposite of productivity was being still. Rest, taking breaks, making time to recharge—all of this fell under the unwanted identity of "idle."

Reflecting on my past, I see that this pattern of misunderstanding and avoiding rest is one of the key factors that eventually landed me in burnout. As a therapist, I've thought a lot about rest and what that can mean for people. In my own journey of integrating rest into my productivity habits, I had to grapple with accepting two things:

1. Overcoming the inaccuracy or misunderstanding of what rest is

2. Becoming aware of the beliefs I held about rest that perpetuate toxic productivity

How do we come to learn the messages about rest that influence our choices? You guessed it: we absorb these ideas about rest from the environment around us, especially those lessons learned in childhood. Even though the message of "resting is not a worthy use of time" was never verbalized within my family, it was everywhere around me. Growing up in an immigrant family, resting felt indulgent, almost luxurious—something reserved for those whose lives could afford it.* Even our weekend recreation activities were focused on learning something: swimming, tennis, classical singing lessons.

Because I was raised to value myself more highly when I am creating, doing, and achieving, any sort of stillness seemed like a threat to my growth. What I didn't know back then was that stillness is actually a part of growth. I learned this lesson by random chance one day when a Google search took me to the website for Seattle's Japanese Garden. I can't even remember how I ended up on that page, but it was there that I came across a concept called *yohaku no bi*. Translated as "the beauty of the space left empty," this concept informs the Zen art practice of leaving empty or negative space as a way to invite balance.

---

* This is not every immigrant family's experience, but it is common due to the socio-demographic and cultural experiences of immigration.

As I reflected on *yohaku no bi*, I realized how much of my life I had spent filling in every moment. After operating within a discrete binary between *doing* and *being* for so long, I had lost all nuance about what it really means to be productive. This simple concept made me see full and empty not as opposites, but as two parts of a whole. Life is a perpetual balancing act between doing and being. In fact, they are two sides of the same coin. To feel satisfied with the life you have, you can't have one without the other.

What's the Connection Between Rest and Toxic Productivity?

The toxic productivity mindset keeps you "on" at all times, constantly engaging in activity and thinking about how to do more or what to do next. This takes a heavy toll on your nervous system, a complex network of nerves that serves as a communication channel between the brain and body.

The nervous system has two settings: sympathetic, which controls your body's stress response, and parasympathetic, which controls your body's relaxation response. When you are stuck in a toxic mindset, you stay in a state of sympathetic nervous system activation. This results in the physical manifestation of burnout: feeling worn down, trouble sleeping, random body aches and pains, difficulty focusing, or changes in appetite. Even more troubling, a chronically activated nervous system can, over time, change the neural pathways that enable relaxation.[60] In other words, the stress caused by toxic productivity is self-perpetuating: our drive to do more makes it physically harder for us to do less.

Burnout

We've touched on burnout—the most extreme end of the toxic productivity spectrum—throughout this book; recall that intense burnout eventually caused me to quit my job at the mental health start-up. This state of exhaustion (physical, mental, and emotional) is caused by prolonged stress and toxic amounts of action without adequate amounts of rest.

Burnout shows up as extreme fatigue, feeling disconnected from others and activities you used to enjoy, and lowered productivity.[61] While the term has been around since the 1970s, it wasn't until 2019 that the World Health Organization officially recognized burnout as a syndrome.[62] Three years later, in 2022, burnout was added to the International Classification of Diseases (ICD-11). While the ICD definition limits the parameters of burnout to work-related stressors, new research is expanding the application of burnout to non-work contexts as well, including being a parent or caregiver, living within a high-demand marriage or romantic relationship, or experiencing systemic social and political stressors.[63,64]

When people are burned out in their relationships or their personal lives, they feel like they must be somehow to blame for it—that they wouldn't feel this way if they were more organized, if they weren't so lazy, or if they were better with time management. While this sentiment is not true, it is very common. I see this mindset frequently in my clients: people pushing themselves too hard yet going on nevertheless, either because they assume it's normal to feel that way (it's not) or else because they believe that they are the only ones struggling to keep up (they're not).

The following are a few red flags that signal the onset of burnout.[65] While this list is not exhaustive or diagnostic, it can help you reflect on whether you've noticed these signs* in yourself, or in a partner or friend (if so, consider checking in with them):

- **You notice a change in sleeping habits:** Are you sleeping too much, waking up in the middle of the night, or having a hard time falling asleep?

- **You feel a different type of tired:** Do you feel ongoing extreme fatigue? Do you wake up tired no matter how early you go to sleep? Do you find yourself getting very tired in the afternoons?

- **You experience "random" health problems:** Do you get headaches for no obvious reason? Have you noticed new digestive issues showing up?

- **You have intensified emotional reactions:** Do you feel more irritable, cynical, or tearful than usual? Have you or others noticed a change in your mood?

- **You withdraw from pleasurable activities:** Do you feel disconnected or disengaged from others and the things that used to give you joy?

- **You feel general apathy:** Are you feeling less committed to your roles at work and in your personal life? Does completing certain tasks (doing laundry, paying bills, shopping for groceries, attending regular healthcare appointments, etc.) feel like it will take a mountainous effort? Are everyday tasks falling to the wayside?

- **You have an overactivated nervous system:** Do you experience an increased heart rate, rapid and shallow breathing, an inability to focus, sweating, or dizziness? Do you always feel "on," even when you have free time?

---

* If you feel like any of these are a significant issue for you, I encourage you to talk to your medical provider for more support.

Sometimes we are aware of the physical, mental, and emotional impairment to our bodies, as they make it difficult to be at our best. But other times, our need for productivity is so strong that we do not notice them until it is too late. This is where the importance of making time for rest comes in.

Rest and Rejuvenation: Why We Need Both

What do you visualize when you think about rest? A nap? Maybe hanging out on the couch? Perhaps taking a warm bath with some candles?

You wouldn't be wrong, but you're not totally right either.

Rest is actually made up of two parts: (1) creating space for doing nothing and (2) engaging in behaviors that actively nourish you. However, I've noticed that when we talk about resting, we tend to only talk about the first part, the "doing nothing" part. Nourishing activities stop being nourishing when they're treated like an item on a checklist. To be effective, nourishing activities must be free from the pressure of outcome and instead be pursued for the sake of joy itself.

This mindset shows up so innocuously in our daily habits that we don't even realize it. I noticed this with Jeremy from the very outset of a session. He walked in the door, dropped himself on the leather couch, and jumped right into giving me a breakdown of his week.

"A bunch of friends came over from Philly, and I had plans every single night," he recounted. "On Thursday, I spent the night in. I told myself I was just going to chill, let my mind 'breathe,' as you say." He gave me a smirk.

By this point, his resistance to fully "buying into" self-care practices while giving them a halfhearted attempt them had become an inside joke between us.

"Ah, okay. How was Thursday evening for you?" I asked, wondering if he spent the evening swiping on dating apps.

"I changed into sweats, ordered Thai, started watching my favorite show, then . . ." Another smirk. "I kind of scrolled on Instagram and TikTok for most of the evening, messaged a few girls here and there to see if they'd respond. Just kept it super low-key."

"Hmm." I gestured for him to continue.

"Well, I just kind of sat around scrolling, and by the time I realized it, it was already 10 p.m.! So I ate quickly—you know I don't love eating late—then hit the bed. Honestly, I didn't feel that 'refreshed.'" He looked at me half accusingly, half apologetically. "What did I do wrong?"

The scenario Jeremy described has happened to me many times. I'll decline an invitation or intentionally leave my schedule open, looking forward to some time for rest, only to fall into mindless activities like social media scrolling or binge-watching a show. Because these activities are passive, they don't fill my cup; in fact, sometimes I feel even more tired afterward than when I started. It's like I've gone through the motions of resting without getting any of the rewards. Oftentimes, I half-wish I'd spent the evening working instead—at least I'd have felt some payoff for my time.

"Let's not think about this in terms of right or wrong," I said. "But we can think about how to do things differently, especially when it feels like what we tried didn't work out. The thing to remember about rest, Jeremy, is that it isn't about just doing nothing. Once we create space for nothingness, we must be intentional about filling that nothingness with energy to inspire and refuel."

He nodded in acknowledgment, but I could tell he was still looking for a concrete answer.

"On Thursday, you might have taken a break from socializing, but did you engage with things that fill your energy reserve?"

"I don't know what 'fills my energy,'" Jeremy confessed.

"Well, what do you like doing?" I pursued. "What kinds of activities light you up or bring you joy?"

He thought for a moment but didn't have an answer. And that, in itself, was his answer: Jeremy needed to discover where he found joy, fulfillment, and passion for his life outside of the checklist that he used to measure his value.

Doing nothing is only the halfway point to rest. The second half is doing something rejuvenating. This can be anything that keeps you present, intentional, and engaged with yourself. Some examples of rejuvenating activities include:

- Spending time in nature or with animals
- Meditating or doing mindfulness exercises
- Expressive writing
- Participating in movement-based activities such as dancing, sports, or stretching
- Crafting or doing any type of creative expression
- Engaging with the arts while being present (watching a movie, listening to music without doing anything else, etc.)
- Making a meal from scratch
- Daydreaming

Make rest and rejuvenation a necessary step within your productivity habits. Rest and productivity have what seems on the surface like a counterintuitive relationship. However, they are not mutually exclusive—they work together. Rest activates the parasympathetic nervous system, allowing for restful sleep, mental clarity, and the reduction of stress hormones in your body. By including rest as something that will *help* you be more productive, you will be able to move toward healthy productivity.

What You Think About Rest Affects Your Ability to Rest

I never really knew the meaning of the phrase "driving on fumes" until one day when I was driving on Highway 1 through California's wine country on a road trip with my partner. A few hours into the drive, the low gas light came on. With only two hours left to get to our destination, we decided to push through. But within the hour, the gas needle had dropped to its last bar, and the closest gas station was 25 miles away. We kept pushing the drive, frantically Googling how many miles you can drive a car when the gas light turns on and trying to ignore all the unrecognizable sounds the car was making.

That's what ignoring rest feels like. You might get all your tasks done, but while you do, you may feel stressed out, exhausted, or barely keeping it together. Most people will push through, riding on fumes and deprioritizing rest, until one day they wind up stranded in the middle of nowhere.

Our unconscious mind is very powerful: we do what we believe, even when we don't know that we believe it. The biggest hurdles to giving ourselves self-care are the beliefs we have about self-care (and rest) in the first place. To get to the root of these beliefs, it's necessary to examine the misconceptions you might have about rest.

One common misconception is thinking that rest is something that must be earned by doing a certain number of actions or reaching a particular achievement. When we are younger, this idea is often reinforced by teachers and parents who use rest activities (naptime, playing with friends, reading, etc.) as an incentive to get work done. When we become older, this mindset becomes a pattern of overcommitting to action and putting rest on a pedestal. In effect, we've made it another achievement milestone that we must prove ourselves worthy of.

Another common misconception about rest is that it will lower your motivation to produce. This belief fits in well within the toxic productivity mindset because it is driven by fear of failure. The anxiety and worry triggered by this fear prevent us from resting.

Many of us also believe that we simply don't have time to rest. This thought makes us believe two things (1) time is a resource that must be put toward productivity, and (2) resting is a waste of time because in the time we are resting, we could instead do something else. These two thoughts combined convince us, in the end, that the rest is not worth it.

But we must recognize that, in some cases, we are genuinely busy or have a really packed calendar that can't be trimmed down. Even in this circumstance, however, you can find time to rest. How? By resting in small increments. You don't have to rest for hours to feel the benefits. You can simply engage in a rejuvenating activity for 10 or 15 minutes a day.

Exercise

What Are Your Thoughts About Rest?

Let's uncover your misconceptions about rest. For the next few minutes, think back to the last time you had free time and were resting. Quickly jot down the first thing that comes to mind when you consider the following questions (don't overthink it):

1. What do you usually say to yourself when you have free time?

2. When you are resting, how does your body feel?

---

3. If someone you know or live with is sitting idle, sleeping in, or not doing anything, what do you say to them? What do you think about them at that moment?

Read over what you've written and become curious about what your thoughts reflect in terms of how you conceptualize rest. Do any of the themes match up to the misconceptions in the previous section, or do they tell you something else?

Rest is a complicated concept in our society today. For some people, rest is a privilege that is inaccessible, whether it be due to lifestyle, social systems, financial constraints, or even access to space. I want to emphasize that my message about rest is not meant to shame or judge anyone. Instead, it is an invitation to think about what rest can look like for you in your specific circumstance.

Different Types of Rest

Because I didn't grow up seeing healthy rest as a part of day-to-day life, I genuinely struggled to know what rest could look like for me. At best, I saw it as a reaction to being too tired to do anything else. At worst, I saw it as a waste of time. As a result, I struggled to identify what would make me feel rested. Instead, I spent a lot of time (and money) doing self-care things that didn't really fit my needs.

I remember one conversation I had with a friend many years ago, before I was a therapist, that changed how I looked at rest. One day, I was on my way to get my nails done, and I was complaining to my friend how much that activity frustrated me.

"It takes so long; you can't do anything else and it's so boring," I said, embarrassed at how whiny I sounded.

"Why are you going then?" she justifiably asked.

"I guess because it makes me feel good about myself?" I replied, half-wondering the same thing.

"You know you don't have to go and spend an hour doing something that annoys you," she said. "Just because it's supposed to make you feel good, doesn't mean it will. Your way of feeling good about yourself doesn't have to look like everyone else's. It should match you—your mood and your energy."

God bless the friends who are willing to tell you the truth. While getting my nails done that day, I thought about what I needed to feel good about myself instead of what I thought was supposed to make me feel good. Over the years, and after much trial and error, I became better attuned to my body, better at identifying my needs and what would really fulfill them.

The same principle applies to finding what kind of rest will nourish you, depending on your mood and energy level, and what's available to you. If you are craving stillness, going for a walk might not be the ideal restful activity; you might be better off meditating, working on a craft, or reading for pleasure. On days you feel more energetic, you might swap the nap for activities like a workout or a lively gathering with friends.

In the book *Sacred Rest*, physician and researcher Dr. Saundra Dalton-Smith outlines six types of rest:[66]

- **Creative rest:** Go walk in nature (unplugged), play with a pet, or lose yourself for a few minutes in a craft, puzzle, or adult coloring book.

- **Social rest:** Spend some time alone, when you are not socializing with anyone (in real life or over social media). Whether you are an extrovert, introvert, or ambivert, everyone needs alone time to be with their thoughts.

- **Mental rest:** Make sure to take breaks during the day, ideally after every 25 minutes of work. Write out your thoughts in a journal in the morning or evening to ease the cognitive pressure on your brain.

- **Sensory de-stimulation rest:** We are stimulated all the time, our senses constantly engaged through things like notifications, music, or sounds of the city around us. Meditations, a short digital detox, or a forest bath* will all help with restoring balance in your senses.

- **Physical rest:** Give your body a break. Take short naps during the day. Stretch daily. Make sure your posture is good throughout the day.

- **Emotional rest:** This means improving your emotional resilience and expanding your ability to sit with difficult emotions. You can use mindfulness activities or speak with a therapist to help with this.

I want to highlight that there is no right or wrong way to rest; there are simply different types of rest, and each one can be helpful, depending on your specific needs at that moment. It is important to think critically about how you engage with rest, so you can make it a part of your life in a healthy way.

Research has shown that decluttering your physical space has a positive effect on mental clarity.[67,68] The same is true for mental decluttering, done best through rest and rejuvenation. The one thing that really helped me change my habits around rest was being intentional about it. This means giving yourself the permission to slow down, even if it feels like the world is moving forward without

---

* Forest bathing, or *shinrin-yoku*, is the practice of spending time in nature, focusing on your senses as they connect with the world around you.

you. Being intentional about rest means actively making sure you have time and resources for it. Here are a few ways I incorporated rest into my life:

- **Schedule it in and treat it like an appointment:** Put your rest time in the calendar and protect that time. You can even make it a recurring event so that you don't have to worry about scheduling it every week.

- **Create a space in your house, workplace, or a public spot that you feel comfortable in (coffee shop, park, etc.) that you go to for rest:** Having a space that makes you feel relaxed and is special to you enhances the experience. It doesn't have to be a big space, but somewhere you feel like you can relax.

- **Plan in advance to take a mental health day:** Once in a while, take a day off from *everything*. This means no errands, no emails, nothing except doing something you really enjoy. (This doesn't have to be a full day; it can be a morning or afternoon.)

- **Set non-negotiable self-care routines:** Taking time for yourself is not an indulgence; it's an absolute priority. For example, fix a time for your lunch, exercise, or reading regularly. Make sure the people in your life are also aware that this is your time.

Rest Rituals

How many times have you made a fresh cup of coffee and started drinking it while checking emails and very quickly forgotten about it, only to find it surprisingly ice cold when you gulp it down? Now imagine making your coffee and sitting down for three minutes before opening your emails. In those three minutes, you smell the coffee, savor the flavor, and maybe let your thoughts drift to how the coffee is grown or to a memory of an enjoyable cup you had on vacation. Perhaps you simply watch the world go by outside your window. Then you turn on your email and dive into work. The end result is the same: you check your email and have a coffee. What's different is the way you get there. The quality of your process makes a difference to how you feel.

In the previous section, we discussed scheduling your rest into your weekly schedule—making a dedicated time (and even a space, if you'd like) for just resting. This intentional plan allows you to be fully present in whatever you are doing. For an even more dedicated rest routine, you can also create what is known as a *rest ritual*. A ritual is a series of small habits that you do regularly and consistently that is connected to a larger goal of yours. Having a ritual around rest is an effective way to integrate it into your daily routine. Regular rest rituals can even have a domino effect on other areas of your life—one positive health habit can encourage you to start another one, creating a cascading effect of increasing overall health and wellness.

Exercise

Creating Your Own Rest Ritual

Let's create a rest ritual. Use the following steps to add something to your schedule that you know calms your body or gives you some space to breathe:

1. Choose a time of day for your ritual (morning, mid-afternoon, or nighttime) that you will keep consistent.

2. Pick one small restorative thing you can easily add to that time—something that won't require you changing your current situation. For example, if you go to the gym after work every day, instead of adding another yoga class (unrealistic), add a three-minute meditation at the end of your workout (realistic).

3. Do that one small thing for four weeks. Keep track of when you successfully complete your ritual on your phone, in a journal, or with an accountability partner.

4. Once the four weeks are over, reflect on the experience. How did you feel after completing this consistently for four weeks? Did you adjust the timing or duration?

5. Reflect on one more thing you can add without disrupting your routine and follow the previous steps with your new ritual.

Rituals can be difficult to implement regularly in the beginning. It's okay if you miss a few days or have an off week; don't let that throw you off track. The idea is simply to maintain consistency as much as possible.

How to Set Boundaries for Rest

Another aspect of incorporating rest into your daily routine is to recognize and be able to implement healthy boundaries. Our boundaries are meant to protect us and help improve our relationships, but because so many of us have a hard time with boundaries, we tend to ignore them altogether. For instance, you may schedule a rest-filled evening on a certain night of the week, but your friends continue to invite you out at this particular time. You don't want to run the risk of them not inviting you anymore, so you abandon your rest altogether.

In the book *Set Boundaries, Find Peace*, author and therapist Nedra Glover Tawwab discusses how setting healthy boundaries improves not only your relationship with others but more importantly, your relationship with yourself.[69] Healthy boundaries are a way to communicate what is and isn't acceptable for you and, by extension, what other people can expect from you. In the previous example, you might communicate to your friends that it is vital for you to get your alone time, but you would be happy to join them every other week or to show up a little later, after you've had time to rest and rejuvenate. Healthy boundaries with yourself are a way to know what your emotional needs are and how to hold yourself accountable.

When we don't have healthy boundaries with ourselves, we run the risk of falling deeper into the toxic productivity mindset. During my work with Maya, I could see her pattern of sacrificing rest was leading her dangerously close to burnout.

"Maya, you've said in the last few sessions that you've had trouble sleeping lately. Can we talk about that a little?" I asked. "I'm wondering what in your life changed around the time you started having sleep issues."

"I think it started around my birthday," she said. "My coworker asked me to help her out with her project and I had to cancel my plans to visit the spa that weekend." She let out a sigh of frustration. "I had that spa credit for months and it expired. I'm so annoyed I didn't go—I just got too busy. Anyway, yeah, I think there's just a lot happening—I'm doing a 10-week financial course, and there's committee work on top of my usual workload. Just life, I guess."

"So, you're doing a lot and that's affecting how you're sleeping. Is there anything you can change right now that you think could make a difference?"

"Honestly, I don't know. I guess I have to figure out what I can cut out . . ." She left her sentence hanging.

"Everything feels important, right?" I completed that thought for her.

She nodded.

"When we feel everything is important, we don't realize how to set the boundaries that can help preserve our emotional energy so we can take care of ourselves," I explained. "Only you can figure out if something is important, urgent, or both, but that requires you to take the time to reflect on it before committing."

"That makes sense, but how do I *do* this?" she sighed, clearly frustrated at her predicament.

"I know it's frustrating, but the good news is that you have the power to change it. Let's start by learning how to identify your boundaries when someone asks you for something or if you feel like committing to something."

In that session, we started working on helping her identify how a boundary violation feels in her body and how she could learn to say no to honor her own commitments. This would eventually make space in her life for rest. Over time, Maya became better at setting healthier boundaries with herself and prioritizing rest, along with the other mindset and habit shifts I've shared in this book, which helped her start to break out of the toxic productivity mindset.

Exercise

Identifying Your Boundaries Around Rest

If you struggle to recognize your own boundaries and it leads you to skip rest, this exercise will help identify your boundaries with a work-life balance, your personal relationships, or with yourself. Use the following strategies to identify certain boundaries you may need to strengthen:

- **Connect with your body:** Most of us will feel a boundary violation before we know that a boundary has been crossed. What happens in your body when a request is made of you? Do your muscles tighten when you see an email notification or a text you weren't expecting? Does your heart begin to race when your someone gives you an extra responsibility? Do any people or types of interactions make your stomach feel strange? Avoid trying to analyze the why behind your discomfort for now—just recognize the pattern.

- **Recognize emotional cues:** Start becoming aware of what emotions come up around certain people, moments, or environments. The four big emotional red flags for a boundary violation are discomfort, fear, resentment, and anger. Again, just identify them for now; don't judge or try to "fix" them.

- **Reflect on the past, your family, childhood, and early relationships:** Our past experiences can give us a strong indication of what boundaries we need in the present. Did the body sensations or emotions you've noted arise when you were growing up? In what situations or with what people did you feel them? Think about your early relationships and your roles in your family. Were you asked to take care of others over taking care of yourself? What happened if you asked for what you needed?

Once you've recognized a boundary that you need to set, you can use the step-by-step plan to say no that we discussed in chapter 9:

1. Thank the person for thinking of you.

2. Ask for time.

3. When you're ready to respond, decline as simply as possible.

4. If you want, offer an alternative.

If the boundary you need to enact is with yourself, buying time becomes even more imperative. The false sense of urgency we explored in chapter 9 shows up strongly when we don't have healthy boundaries with ourselves. This can lead to overcommitting, overworking, and eventually experiencing burnout. So, when you feel tempted to jump into something, learn to practice pausing and giving yourself some time to reflect on whether you have the emotional and time capacity to commit to it.

At its core, rest is about rebuilding your connection to yourself. It creates space for you to hear the messages your body and emotions are giving you and an opportunity to reclaim your time in a way that is nourishing.

The Healing Power of Blank Spaces

There were times when I was writing this book when I felt incredibly stuck. In those moments, my inner critic was activated, and I experienced almost every emotion that we have explored in the previous chapters: shame, guilt, perfectionism, comparison, and a whole host of other feelings. There were days when I spent two or three hours staring at my screen, unable to write. I would turn to "busy work" like reading articles, scrolling social media, or organizing my desktop to distract myself from the negative self-talk that was saying, *You're not writing fast enough; this is not good enough; you are not good enough.*

What made it even more frustrating was that I couldn't predict when such a dry spell would come. Not knowing when I would have a "bad writing day" started giving me anxiety. As a way to cope, I started paying attention to when it happened and eventually noticed that my writing paralysis was always preceded by a few days when I did not practice rest, but instead was working until 8 p.m., going to bed late and forcing myself to wake up early, having too many back-to-back meetings, and generally not taking any breaks (physical or mental).

On the other hand, I noticed that my best writing days came in the weeks where I intentionally scheduled fun activities and empty time slots in my calendar. This was because I was giving myself the time to rest—to let my mind wander, to not be stimulated by thoughts and activities, and to engage in fulfilling self-care activities. This led to an uptick in my creativity, allowing me to approach my writing from a place of refreshed calmness.

That's the power of rest. It allows you to show up for your goals from a healthy place. In the book *How to Do Nothing: Resisting the Attention Economy,* author and artist Jenny Odell discusses a fable told by the ancient Chinese philosopher Zhuang Zhou about a tree so crooked and twisted that the loggers considered it not worth cutting down.[70] The tree, in return, points out how its perceived uselessness allows it to continue living, bearing fruit, and providing shade. A phrase Odell used struck a deep chord with me: "the usefulness of uselessness." So many people think resting is useless, and because we see it that way, we don't recognize or experience its benefits. There are times the most powerful opportunity for personal growth lies in making more space for "uselessness" in our lives. Sometimes the things we think have no purpose are, indeed, the things that hold the greatest power to heal us.

Key Takeaways

- Resting is part of the productivity process, and over time it makes your ability to be productive more sustainable.

- Without rest, you can experience burnout, which causes you to feel extremely tired, disconnect from others, and lessen your productivity.

- There are many different types of rest, but all rest consists of two parts: doing nothing and doing something to rejuvenate yourself.

- Incorporating rest into your routine is made easier if you schedule appointments or daily rituals. Sometimes, these "empty spaces" provide just what we need to move forward.

- Having healthy boundaries lets you communicate to others what is and isn't acceptable for you regarding time for rest and rejuvenation.

Chapter 11

Reimagining Productivity

"Stepping out of busyness, stopping our endless pursuit of getting somewhere else, is perhaps the most beautiful offering we can make to our spirit."

—**Tara Brach, *True Refuge: Finding Peace and Freedom in Your Own Awakened Heart***

"I've been doing a lot of thinking about what we've discussed."

Jeremy sat down at the start of one of our sessions, tapping his knee with his fingers. Intrigued by this announcement, I waved at him to continue.

"You know how we've talked about figuring out what I really value in a potential partner?" he began tentatively, his fingers still drumming his knee.

I wonder what he's so anxious about, I thought to myself, half-expecting him to confess something extreme like he's giving up on love or that he has decided that therapy wasn't working for him (again).

Instead, he said, "Well, I've been trying to do that."

"It is important to think about these things," I said, offering him some validation. "It shows you care about yourself."

"That's the thing!" he said. "I don't really have time to care about myself or think about what I want or what is important to me. Even when I'm home, I'm not really thinking. It's almost like I don't want to think about this. I'm afraid, I think . . ." He paused, closing his eyes. Then, as fast as he could, he blurted, "I'm afraid I'll find out that I don't know what I want or what I'm even doing. And now that I'm saying this out loud, I feel like I've just wasted so much of my life chasing the perfect girl and trying to meet my stupid checklist . . . and what if she doesn't even exist? What am I even doing?"

This word-vomiting was a genuine breakthrough. Jeremy had let down his defenses and was willing to change his outlook and his habits.

"All right!" I said, smiling. "First, let's take a breath. There are a few different things you're saying right now, and it all feels like one giant blob because all the things have gotten jumbled up. Let's take it one thought at a time. Why don't you take out your phone to take some notes as we're talking."

After taking a few deep breaths, we began to deconstruct his breakthrough.

"This is a significant shift, even if it feels scary or overwhelming," I said. "It sounds like connection is becoming more important to you, over . . . let's say, the numbers?"

"Yes—is that normal? I've spent so much time playing this numbers dating game, and do you remember that girl I went out with a few weeks ago? I didn't even like her! I'm starting to feel like . . . like an emptiness in that."

"It's not weird," I assured him. "You're recognizing your emotional needs, and you're realizing that you have to make time for *you*." I paused to let that sink in. "I'm curious, how do you imagine incorporating this mindset shift into your dating life now?"

"Honestly, I have to do what you said to me like months ago . . ." He looked at me sheepishly. "I bet this happens a lot. You say something and then your client realizes it months later."

"Most people know what they need to do; they're just not ready for it," I answered. "I think you also knew this deep inside. And now you're ready to do it, which is fantastic!"

"I need to slow down, be more selective, spend some time alone, and I guess, I don't really know what I like or what I don't like. I want to get to know myself a little more. It's still scary that I keep coming back to 'What if I miss out on someone good?' But we both know that hasn't helped me so far. I can't keep living like this." He ended with a wan smile.

"That's a great starting point, Jeremy. Remember, it's not about missing out; it's about gaining something real and fulfilling. Look at this as an opportunity to explore meaningful connections at a slower pace, so you can make space for genuine relationships."

With that, Jeremy entered a new era of his dating life: breaking out of his toxic productivity approach to dating—instead focusing on connecting with his values to guide his habits.

Change can be intimidating, but the fact that you have this book (and that you are this far into it!) means you are willing to make changes regarding your productivity. Perhaps you have a good idea of where you need to go, or maybe you're still contemplating where you'd like to be. That's okay! You must approach change with a balance that feels right for you. This is what reimagining productivity means—not abandoning productivity, but rather finding a balance between doing and not doing.

Reimagining productivity is learning to question the frameworks we believe about achievement and self-worth. Like Lara, who had to question her belief that living the most optimized life meant living a worthy life. Or like Margaret, who believed that being productive was the key to love and approval. Or Sarah, who believed that packing her schedule with work and social commitments would make her feel as good as her friends. In this chapter, we will wrap up with my clients, finding out how they embraced the reimagining of toxic productivity and how you can too.

The Most Optimized Life Is Not the Happiest Life

We know productivity culture is obsessed with hyper-optimization: trying to make the most of every waking hour toward outcomes, achievement, and productivity. This cultural obsession is reflected in the influx of new products, services, and apps launching every day to help us become more productive and efficient. As diverse as they might seem, they all have one underlying message: *There is one right way to live and be productive, and the way you're doing it now isn't it.*

Since we all want to live our best life, the notion of optimization is incredibly seductive, especially for people oriented toward ambition and achievement. Lara struggled with this question, plagued by wondering if she was doing the most, in the best way possible, for herself, her kids, and her career. While replacing her inner critic with her inner coach and learning to identify unhelpful thought patterns was imperative for Lara in healing her toxic productivity, releasing herself from the myth of optimization was a crucial step.

While a planned and structured life may help you achieve the things you want, it removes any possibility of surprise or discovery. This happens because an extremely structured life with no space for spontaneity generates the same types of experiences over and over again. On the other hand, leaving room for spontaneity provides the potential to open yourself up to new experiences. This will expand your perspectives and give you more opportunities for growth. New experiences give you the chance to learn something different; you might learn something new about yourself, your loved ones, or even the world around you. This is what Lara experienced when she started creating pockets of empty space in her schedule to spend time with her husband and their children.

"Over the last four weeks, your homework has been to have empty blocks in your schedule: one weeknight and once over the weekend. How are you feeling about it?" I asked Lara.

"I'm embarrassed to say . . ." She hesitated before diving in. "I'm learning so much about my kids' lives! What they're doing in school, their friend dramas, and just little things I've never heard about. Also, we've got a weekly game night with the kids now, and after they go to bed, Sam and I spend the evening together. It's nice—it just sucks that I didn't think about this before."

"That's an amazing insight, Lara. You should feel so proud of yourself for leaning into making a change that felt scary, and now you can see how great it feels!" I said, delighted for her progress.

"You know," Lara ventured, "I was thinking about something you said to me once—that our feelings are like messengers. I was talking to Sam about it, and I realized that I feel embarrassed about not knowing my kids better, but I think that feeling is telling me something: it is important for me to have connection with my family. It's weird—I still wake up with anxiety on weekends because I know I could be doing things, but then I remind myself that 'empty time' is where I build connection with Sam and the kids, and it makes me feel better."

"I am certain you'll find a balance between the things you want to do as achievements and the things you want to feel as connections," I assured her.

By loosening her optimized, highly structured schedule, Lara was able to find a new opportunity to connect with her family. It also gave her the chance to reflect on what type of mother she really wanted to be and how she wanted her family life to look, instead of letting a checklist dictate this for her.

Are We Productive or Are We Just Busy?

Another important step in reimagining productivity is being able to distinguish between being busy and being productive. This was the next step in Margaret's journey to heal her toxic productivity. In mistaking a packed calendar for a productive calendar, Margaret had conflated two ideas: *I need to be productive to be of value to others* and *Being busy means I am being productive.* When I brought up these conflated ideas, she met me with a blank, uncomprehending stare.

"The biggest distinction between being busy and being productive is that being busy is a reactive approach to your tasks," I explained. "You are responding to things that need your attention. Being productive is a proactive approach to your tasks and life—it has more intention toward a larger goal."

Margaret nodded intently.

"Productivity is defined by the importance and impact of the actions we take, not just completing the action," I continued. "In other words, we measure success not by the number of tasks completed but by the impact of those tasks on our overall goals or purpose. That's why we call the stuff that keeps us busy 'busywork'—it refers to little tasks that don't really have a large impact." Based on Margaret's expression,

I wasn't sure how convincing this was for her. "Is this resonating with you?"

"I see what you're saying, and it's not that I don't agree with you," she replied. "I just don't think it's possible for me to take on any less or say no when my boss calls on me. I need to find a way to feel happy and content within that, you know?"

"I can understand that making changes feels impossible right now," I assured her. "We can definitely keep our focus on helping you develop coping skills to manage how you're feeling."

Margaret was in the middle of her journey, at what is known as the contemplation stage of change. When we are in the contemplation stage of change, we consider the pros and cons of changing habits versus staying within the same patterns. Before she could make the shift, she would need to see for herself that there is an alternative to a fast-paced, action-packed life.

Intentional Living

In a world that is constantly asking for our attention and resources to do more, the most radical thing we can do is turn our attention and resources inward. By going inward, we become better able to connect with the outer world, the community we live in. Slowing down the toxic productivity cycle requires us to become more intentional about our choices and where we spend our time and energy.

The toxic mindset believes that doing nothing is a waste of time, so our default state of being becomes to move as fast as possible through life. We think two steps ahead, trying to multitask and race through our checklist. We go from one milestone to the next, acting quickly and taking on too much. This is something that came up in my sessions with Sarah quite often.

"Sarah, based on the things we've been talking about over these past few months—you feeling too busy, overwhelmed, and disconnected from your friends—I wanted to bring up a concept that I think might be helpful, or at least interesting, to you, if you're open to it," I said at the beginning of the session.

She nodded, clicking her pen as it hovered above her journal.

"Can you think of something you could change about your daily habits to incorporate some intentionality into it?"

"I thought *you* were going to tell me something!" She laughed and then said, "I guess? I don't know . . . why would I do that?"

"Building a practice of intentionality helps us become more present in life by being deliberate and focused when making a decision," I explained. "It means considering the importance versus impact of our decisions."

"How will this help me feel better?" she asked, sounding curious but wary.

"Cultivating intentionality in your life will help you break out of the overcommitting mindset and ease up the comparisons to others," I explained. "This will help you recognize that you do have the power to shape your life through the decisions you make, instead of feeling like you are on the receiving end of other people's decisions. It will give you a sense of personal direction so you can feel more present in your life."

"I understand what you're saying," she said, pointing the pen at her head. Then she added, "But I don't understand what you're saying," she said, then pointing the pen at her heart.

"So, sometimes you say yes to things too quickly, right?" I prompted. "Intentional living would mean asking for time to think about the request before you say yes. It would mean thinking about whether the request is genuinely aligned with your values and your goals, and considering the potential impact of saying yes versus saying no."

"Okay, I get it a little." She hesitated. "I feel like it'll be hard though."

"Of course," I agreed. "Anything new is difficult to do. Obviously, these changes are easier for us to discuss in a session, and they're much more difficult for you to implement in real life. But that's why we start small whenever we change a habit or mindset. The changes you make to your productivity habits don't have to be large and all-encompassing. They can be small, and you can make them in an incremental, steady way. The way you make the change is teaching you how to make the change."

Jotting down some notes, Sarah agreed to give this a try. In our time together, she continued to work on slowly incorporating small adjustments in her schedule and habits as a part of her personal growth. Cultivating intentionality in her life helped Sarah reframe the way she looked at herself in relation to others. Over time, she began to reimagine what productivity could look like for her.

Rewriting Your Life Story

In the beginning of this book, I pointed out the importance of sharing our stories, as it is one of the best ways we can grasp our place in the world. Psychologist and philosopher Alice Morgan agrees with me on this, saying, "We give meanings to our experiences constantly as we live our lives. A narrative is like a thread that weaves the events together, forming a story."[71] This perspective offers a way to look at your life: as a story that you have the power to write (and rewrite) as you grow and evolve.

We all have a life story that consists of two parts: (1) what happened to us and (2) how we perceive what happened. What happened to us is based on observable facts about the events of our life, both positive and negative. How we perceive what happened to us is based on a reflection of our early childhood experiences, the messages we have learned and internalized from our caregivers and society, our own self-worth, and other emotional dynamics, all of which we have explored together in this book. While we cannot change the actual events that we've experienced, we do have the power to change our perception of them, including the narrative we believe about who we are and what is possible for us.

Healing toxic productivity through reframing your personal narrative first requires grappling with uncomfortable truths about yourself and facing the need to grow beyond your established patterns. After all, you can't change something you aren't aware of. In addition, you must look at the subjective parts of your belief system. This means examining what you believe to be true from an objective lens and stepping back to reflect on the facts of your circumstances. With all this information, you can create an alternate reimagining of what could *also* be true. This allows you to construct a new perspective on the circumstances you have experienced. It's important to know that reframing your narrative is not questioning the validity of what happened to you or how you felt about it. Rather, it is encouraging yourself to find more than one meaning behind what happened. This allows you to develop deeper understanding of your situation, not just from your perspective, but from different perspectives as well. When you can see these alternate perspectives, it changes how you feel about yourself in relation to your circumstances.

Some ways you can practice reframing the narrative is through self-reflection. For example, consider a perspective you have about yourself or a situation you were in, and then ask yourself:

1. If a third person were to describe or approach the situation, what would they say?

2. Are you examining the other person's experience, motivations, and circumstance as well?

3. What assumptions are underlying your perspective?

4. Could there be a different way to approach this situation?

Key Takeaways

- By loosening an optimized and highly structured idea of productivity, you can make space for spontaneity and surprise in your life, which will enhance the quality of your experiences.

- When making a decision, being intentional helps us to be more present, deliberate, and focused so that we have the opportunity to reflect on whether the choice we make will align with our values, goals, and purpose.

- Being busy is not the same thing as being productive. Productivity is not measured by the number of tasks you complete, but by the impact of those tasks on your overall goals or purpose.

- Reimagining productivity starts with learning to question the frameworks we believe about self-worth, belonging, and achievement.

Chapter 12

Finding a Way
Back to Yourself

"We go on in vices, not because we find satisfaction in it,
but because we are unacquainted with the joys of virtue."

—Mary Astell, *A Serious Proposal to the Ladies*

Breaking out of the toxic productivity mindset requires a paradigm shift within yourself and within your world. I noticed two responses when I started to change my habits. One was resistance: several people in my life met my attempts to be intentional with discouragement or dismissal. This said more about their internalization of productivity and achievement than it did about mine. The second response was from the people who felt an implicit permission to do the same as I'd done: to slow down, to say no, to be intentional. When we see someone from within our community begin to model a healthier relationship with productivity and let it inspire us to find more genuine and gentle ways of living, that's collective healing. It gives me hope that through our own small changes, we will ultimately heal the wounds of our communities.

Close to the end of writing this book, I went to dinner with a friend. She asked me, "So, how's the book going?"

I took a second's pause to decide whether to be truthful or to gloss over it.

"It's been hard," I ultimately said. "I feel like I'm a jack-of-all-trades—I've been doing so many disparate things but not focusing on any one specifically."

My friend looked at me and very hesitantly said, "Israa, do you think that you . . . are struggling with toxic productivity as you write this book?"

The moment suspended us somewhere between honest and awkward, until I burst into laughter, not because what she said was funny, but because it was so absurdly true.

I share this because it's important for you to know this book has been written by someone who is there in the trenches with you. Together, we have identified unhelpful thought patterns, habits, and narratives that we believe about ourselves, productivity, and our self-worth. I hope that you've picked up a few ideas and practices that will help you redefine your relationship with productivity. I also want you to pause and take a moment to thank yourself for sticking with a commitment you made when you picked up this book to read. Just as I am with my clients, I'm honored to walk alongside you on this journey.

Remember, healing is not a linear process, nor is it an all-or-nothing state of being. No matter how strong your self-worth becomes, there will be times when old thought patterns come up, triggered by a difficult life event or a person from your past. Be assured that experiencing a negative thought about yourself doesn't mean all the work you've done has been a waste. Healing yourself doesn't mean never feeling pain again or not having thoughts that get in your way. Healing means that the things that caused you pain no longer overwhelm you, and that you no longer accept negative thoughts as truths.

Who Can You Become?

In the book *The Writing Life*, author Annie Dillard writes, "How we spend our days is, of course, how we spend our lives."[72] I happened upon this quote many years ago and it has stayed with me ever since, sometimes as my phone screensaver, sometimes as an idea for a tattoo, sometimes as a journal prompt to reflect on. For me, it is a reminder to focus on the now, because the now is what ultimately compounds to become your whole life.

I am deeply cognizant of the fact that the decision to feel good in the now goes against the norm. That's what makes it one of the most radical things we can do today. Toxic productivity is the quiet whisper that is urging you to always be in the next place, the next stage, closer to the conclusion. But living this way takes you out of the present; it keeps joy at a distance.

As we move through the different stages of life, we can begin to lose parts of ourselves and attempt to replace them with parts that we think others will respect or accept. But in that process, we become disconnected from ourselves. I invite you to think about the parts of you that you've lost when your passions were replaced with productivity. Decoupling your self-worth from what you do is the first step in coming home to yourself—that is, staking your right to simply exist in a society that wants you to produce until the very end.

One way to return home to yourself is to be intentional about getting to know yourself better. That's why so many of the reflections in this book are about improving self-awareness, bringing attention to your behavioral and emotional patterns, and building a stronger relationship with yourself. Investing in a relationship with ourselves is the only way we can have other meaningful relationships and experiences. This thought has always helped me remember that

I am more than what I produce. When I focus on the things that make me feel grounded and joyful, I am reminded that life contains so much more than the next milestone on my list. The clarity we get by separating our self from our "doing" gives us breathing room to become more aligned with our values and happiness. This has been my hope in writing this book: to inspire you to live a more aligned, connected, and purposeful life, a life too big for a checklist to hold.

I will leave you with one more beautiful piece of writing that has fundamentally changed the way I approach my work. This excerpt from Jennifer Michael Hecht's poem "On the Strength of All Conviction and the Stamina of Love" illustrates how important it is to know when it is time to simply let the sun set.[73]

> But they didn't fill
>
> the desert with pyramids.
>
> They just built some. Some.
>
> They're not still out there,
>
> building them now. Everyone,
>
> everywhere, gets up and goes home.

I hope that someday you are able to clear your mind completely, set your to-do list aside for a while, and bask in the warm glow of your own sunset.

Endnotes

1   "Burnout," *APA Dictionary of Psychology*, last modified April 19, 2018, https://dictionary.apa.org/burnout.

2   *"This Is Water* by David Foster Wallace," *Farnam Street*, https://fs.blog /david-foster-wallace-this-is-water.

3   Judith S. Beck, *Cognitive Behavior Therapy: Basics and Beyond,* 2nd ed. (New York: Guilford Press, 2011).

4   Beck, *Cognitive Behavior Therapy.*

5   Jenna LeJeune and Jason B. Luoma, *Values in Therapy: A Clinician's Guide to Helping Clients Explore Values, Increase Psychological Flexibility & Live a More Meaningful Life* (Oakland: Context Press, 2019).

6   Anthony Patt and Richard Zeckhauser, "Action Bias and Environmental Decisions," *Journal of Risk and Uncertainty* 21, no. 1 (2000): 45–72. https://doi.org/10.1023/A:1026517309871.

7   Kunal Jethuri, "Pareto Principle: The Law of the Vital Few," *Medium*, January 26, 2023, https://medium.com/@igniobydigitate/pareto-principle -the-law-of-the-vital-few-e10d3123eea5.

8   Theodore P. Zanto and Adam Gazzaley, "Aging of the Frontal Lobe," *Handbook of Clinical Neurology* 163 (2019): 369–389, https://doi.org /10.1016/B978-0-12-804281-6.00020-3.

9   Kevin P. Madore and Anthony D. Wagner, "Multicosts of Multitasking," *Cerebrum* (March–April 2019), https://www.ncbi.nlm.nih.gov/pmc /articles/PMC7075496.

10 C. W. and A. J. K. D., "Get a Life," *The Economist*, September 24, 2013, https://www.economist.com/free-exchange/2013/09/24/get-a-life.

11 Nathaniel Kleitman, "Basic Rest-Activity Cycle—22 Years Later," *Sleep* 5, no. 4 (September 1982): 311–317, https://doi.org/10.1093/sleep/5.4.311.

12 Behavior Institute, "Night Owls and Early Birds: Surviving in the World of Morning People," *Medium*, September 27, 2019, https://medium.com /@behaviorinstitute.tr/night-owls-and-early-birds-surviving-in-the-world -of-morning-people-6fdbf627c6b7.

13 Abraham H. Maslow, "A Theory of Human Motivation," *Psychological Review* 50, no. 4 (1943): 370–396, https://doi.org/10.1037/h0054346.

14 Scott Barry Kaufman, *Transcend: The New Science of Self-Actualization* (New York: TarcherPerigee, 2020).

15 Ulrich Orth and Richard Robins, "The Development of Self-Esteem," *Current Directions in Psychological Science* 23, no. 5 (July 2014): 381–387, https://doi.org/10.1177/0963721414547414.

16 "Self-Esteem," *APA Dictionary of Psychology*, updated on November 15, 2023, https://dictionary.apa.org/self-esteem.

17 Eliot R. Smith, Diane M. Mackie, and Heather M. Claypool, *Social Psychology*, 3rd ed. (New York: Psychology Press, 2014).

18 Orth and Robins, "The Development of Self-Esteem."

19 "Self-Worth," *APA Dictionary of Psychology*, updated on November 15, 2023, https://dictionary.apa.org/self-worth.

20 Christina M. Alberini, "Long-Term Memories: The Good, the Bad, and the Ugly," *Cerebrum* (2010): 1–13.

21 Orth and Robins, "The Development of Self-Esteem."

22 Ulrich Orth, Ruth Y. Erol, and Eva C. Luciano, "Development of Self-Esteem from Age 4 to 94 Years: A Meta-Analysis of Longitudinal Studies," *Psychological Bulletin* 144, no. 10 (2018): 1045–1080, https://doi.org/10.1037 /bul0000161.

23 Michael J. Sandel, *The Tyranny of Merit* (New York: Farrar, Straus and Giroux, 2020).

24 Michelle Obama, *Becoming* (New York: Crown, 2018).

25 June P. Tangney, Jeffrey Stuewig, and Andres G. Martinez, "Two Faces of Shame: Understanding Shame and Guilt in the Prediction of Jail Inmates' Recidivism," Psychological Science 25, no. 3 (2014): 799–805, https://doi.org/10.1177/0956797613508790.

26 Jessica L. Tracy and Richard W. Robbins, "Putting the Self Into Self-Conscious Emotions: A Theoretical Model," *Psychological Inquiry* 15, no. 2 (2004): 103–125, https://ubc-emotionlab.ca/wp-content/files_mf/publishedtargetarticle.pdf.

27 Joaquin Selva, "Why Shame and Guilt Are Functional for Mental Health," *Positive Psychology,* January 22, 2018, https://positivepsychology.com/shame-guilt.

28 Tangney, Stuewig, and Martinez, "Two Faces of Shame."

29 Stephanie Alberico, et al., "Guilt and Shame Elicitors: Unwanted Identities, Responsibility, and Interpersonal Consequences" (Presentation, Joint Meeting of the Western and Rocky Mountain Psychological Associations, Albuquerque, NM, April 1998), https://doi.org/10.13140/RG.2.2.13191.80805.

30 Brené Brown, *I Thought It Was Just Me (But It Isn't)* (New York: Gotham, 2014).

31 Brené Brown, *Daring Greatly* (New York: Avery, 2012).

32 Tamara J. Ferguson, Heidi L. Eyre, and Michael Ashbaker, "Unwanted Identities: A Key Variable in Shame-Anger Links and Gender Differences in Shame," *Sex Roles* 42 (2000): 133–157, https://doi.org/10.1023/A:1007061505251.

33 Joachim Stoeber, "The Dual Nature of Perfectionism in Sports: Relationships with Emotion, Motivation, and Performance," *International Review of Sport and Exercise Psychology* 4, no. 2 (2011): 128–145, https://doi.org/10.1080/1750984X.2011.604789.

34 Thomas Curran and Andrew P. Hill, "Perfectionism Is Increasing Over Time: A Meta-Analysis of Birth Cohort: Differences from 1989 to 2016," *Psychological Bulletin* 145, no. 4 (2019): 410–429, https://doi.org/10.1037/bul0000138.

35 Fushcia M. Sirois and Danielle S. Molnar, "Perfectionistic Strivings and Concerns Are Differentially Associated with Self-Rated Health Beyond Negative Affect," *Journal of Research in Personality* 70 (2017): 73–83, https://doi.org/10.1016/j.jrp.2017.06.003.

36 Martin M. Smith, et al., "The Perniciousness of Perfectionism: A Meta-Analytic Review of the Perfectionism-Suicide Relationship," *Journal of Personality* 86, no. 3 (2018): 522–542, https://doi.org/10.1111/jopy.12333.

37 Curran and Hill, "Perfectionism Is Increasing."

38 Curran and Hill, "Perfectionism Is Increasing."

39 Patrick Gaudreau et al., "Because Excellencism Is More Than Good Enough: On the Need to Distinguish the Pursuit of Excellence from the Pursuit of Perfection," *Journal of Personality and Social Psychology* 122, no. 6 (2022): 1117–1145, https://doi.org/10.1037/pspp0000411.

40 Amy Summerville and Neal J. Roese, "Dare to Compare: Fact-Based versus Simulation-Based Comparison in Daily Life," *Journal of Experimental Social Psychology* 44, no. 3 (2008): 664–671, https://doi.org/10.1016/j.jesp.2007.04.002.

41 Jennifer Lewallen and Elizabeth Behm-Morawitz, "Pinterest or Thinterest?: Social Comparison and Body Image on Social Media," *Social Media and Society* 2, no. 1 (2016), https://doi.org/10.1177/2056305116640559.

42 Ravi Chandra, *Facebuddha: Transcendence in the Age of Social Networks* (San Francisco: Pacific Heart Books, 2017).

43 Chris Duffy, "How to Redefine Your Self-Worth (with Meag-gan O'Reilly)," March 2021, in *How to Be a Better Person*, produced by TED and PRX, podcast, MP3 audio, 28:35, https://play.prx.org/listen?ge=prx_357_d20c4a65-8ff7-40d6-b5e6-cfb6112192e6&uf=https%3A%2F%2Ffeeds.feedburner.com%2FHowToBeABetterHuman.

44 Ethan Kross, *Chatter: The Voice in Our Head, Why It Matters, and How to Harness It* (New York: Crown, 2021).

45 Nancy Balaban, "Seeing the Child, Knowing the Person," in *To Become a Teacher* (New York: Teachers College Press, 1996), 52.

46 Beck, *Cognitive Behavior Therapy*.

47 Stephen R. Covey, *The Seven Habits of Highly Effective People: Restoring the Character Ethic* (New York: Free Press, 2004).

48 Wendy Jansen, "Abundance in Positive Design: Part A: The Image of 'Unlimited Good,'" *Academia*, https://www.academia.edu/184001/Abundance_and_scarcity_thinking_and_Design_of_Organizations_and_Networks.

49 Jiaying Zhao and Brandon M. Tomm, "Psychological Responses to Scarcity," *Oxford Research Encyclopedias*, February 26, 2018, https://doi.org/10.1093/acrefore/9780190236557.013.41.

50 Covey, *The Seven Habits*, 219.

51 Theodore Masters-Waage et al., "A Scarcity Mindset Reduces Salary Goals through Lowering Employment Self-Efficacy," *Academy of Management Proceedings*, no. 1 (2022), https://doi.org/10.5465 /AMBPP.2022.13753abstract.

52 Zhao and Tomm, "Psychological Responses to Scarcity."

53 Sendhil Mullainathan and Eldar Shafir, *Scarcity: Why Having Too Little Means So Much* (New York: Times Books, 2013).

54 Zhao and Tomm, "Psychological Responses to Scarcity."

55 Ariel Kalil, Susan Mayer, and Rohen Shah, "Scarcity and Inattention," *Becker Friedman Institute for Economics*, no. 2022-76 (June 2023), https://ssrn.com/abstract=4138637.

56 Anuj K. Shah et al., "Some Consequences of Having Too Little," *Science* 338, no. 682 (2012), https://doi.org/10.1126/science.1222426.

57 Latrina T. Geyer et al., "An Abundance Mindset Approach to Support Nurse Well-Being: The Feasibility of Peer Support," *Nurse Leader* 21, no. 4 (August 2023): 489–493, https://doi.org/10.1016/j.mnl.2023.03.013.

58 Gail Elliott Patricolo et al., "Beneficial Effects of Guided Imagery or Clinical Massage on the Status of Patients in a Progressive Care Unit," *Critical Care Nurse* 37, no. 1 (2017): 62-69, https://doi.org/10.4037 /ccn2017282.

59 Viktor Frankl, *Man's Search for Meaning* (1946; Boston: Beacon Press, 2006).

60 Kaitlyn Miller, "Discussing the Harms of Toxic Productivity with an Expert Psychologist," *Grey Journal*, 2021, https://greyjournal.net/hustle/grow /discussing-the-harms-of-toxic-productivity-with-an-expert-psychologist.

61 "Depression: What Is Burnout," *National Library of Medicine*, last modified June 18, 2020, https://www.ncbi.nlm.nih.gov/books/NBK279286.

62 Herbert J. Freudenberger, "Staff Burn-Out," *Journal of Social Issues* 30 (1974): 159–165, https://doi.org/10.1111/j.1540-4560.1974.tb00706.x.

63 "Burnout," *International Classification of Diseases*, https://icd.who.int /browse11/l-m/en#/http://id.who.int/icd/entity/129180281.

64 Renzo Bianchi et al., "Is Burnout Solely Job-Related? A Critical Comment," *Scandinavian Journal of Psychology* 55, no. 4 (2014): 357–361, https://doi .org/10.1111/sjop.12119.

65 Melinda Wenner Moyer, "Your Body Knows You're Burned Out," *The New York Times*, February 15, 2022, https://www.nytimes.com/2022/02/15/well /live/burnout-work-stress.html.

66 Saundra Dalton-Smith, *Sacred Rest: Recover Your Life, Renew Your Energy, Restore Your Sanity* (New York: Faithwords, 2017).

67 Martin Lang et al., "Effects of Anxiety on Spontaneous Ritualized Behavior," *Current Biology* 25, no. 14 (2015): 1892–1897, https://doi .org/10.1016/j.cub.2015.05.049.

68 Stephanie McMains and Sabine Kastner, "Interactions of Top-Down and Bottom-Up Mechanisms in Human Visual Cortex," *Journal of Neuroscience* 31, no. 2 (2011): 587–597, https://doi.org/10.1523 /JNEUROSCI.3766-10.2011.

69 Nedra Glover Tawwab, *Set Boundaries, Find Peace: A Guide to Reclaiming Yourself* (New York: TarcherPerigee, 2021).

70 Jenny Odell, *How to Do Nothing: Resisting the Attention Economy* (New York: Melville House, 2019).

71 Alice Morgan, *What Is Narrative Therapy? An Easy-to-Read Introduction* (Adelaide, SA: Dulwich Centre Publications, 2000).

72 Annie Dillard, *The Writing Life* (New York: Harper Collins, 1989).

73 Jennifer Michael Hecht, "On the Strength of All Conviction and the Stamina of Love," in *The Next Ancient World* (North Adams, MA: Tupelo Press, 2001).

References

Alberico, Stephanie, Michelle Anderson, Blair Hacker, Aaron Highley, Veronique Marolais, Mendie Moyes, Dane Peterson et al. "Guilt and Shame Elicitors: Unwanted Identities, Responsibility, and Interpersonal Consequences." Presentation, Joint Meeting of the Western and Rocky Mountain Psychological Associations, Albuquerque, NM. April 1998. https://doi.org/10.13140/RG.2.2.13191.80805.

Alberini, Christina M. "Long-Term Memories: The Good, the Bad, and the Ugly." *Cerebrum* (September 2010): 1–13.

APA Dictionary of Psychology. "Burnout." Last modified April 19, 2018. https://dictionary.apa.org/burnout.

APA Dictionary of Psychology. "Self-Esteem." Last modified November 15, 2023. https://dictionary.apa.org/self-esteem.

APA Dictionary of Psychology. "Self-Worth." Last modified November 15, 2023. https://dictionary.apa.org/self-worth.

Balaban, Nancy. "Seeing the Child, Knowing the Person." In *To Become a Teacher*, by William Ayers. New York: Teachers College Press, 1996.

Beck, Judith S. *Cognitive Behavior Therapy: Basics and Beyond.* 2nd ed. New York: Guilford Press, 2011.

Behavior Institute. "Night Owls and Early Birds: Surviving in the World of Morning People." Medium, September 27, 2019, https://medium.com/@behaviorinstitute.tr/night-owls-and-early-birds-surviving-in-the-world-of-morning-people-6fdbf627c6b7.

Bianchi, Renzo, Didier Truchot, Eric Laurent, Romain Brisson, and Irvin Sam Schonfeld. "Is Burnout Solely Job-Related? A Critical Comment." *Scandinavian Journal of Psychology* 55, no. 4 (2014): 357–361. https://doi.org/10.1111/sjop.12119.

Brown, Brené. *Daring Greatly.* New York: Avery, 2012.

Brown, Brené. *I Thought It Was Just Me (But It Isn't)*. New York: Gotham, 2014.

C. W. and A. J. K. D. "Get a Life." *The Economist*, September 24, 2013. https://www.economist.com/free-exchange/2013/09/24/get-a-life.

Chandra, Ravi. *Facebuddha: Transcendence in the Age of Social Networks*. San Francisco: Pacific Heart Books, 2017.

Covey, Stephen R. *The Seven Habits of Highly Effective People: Restoring the Character Ethic*. New York: Free Press, 2004.

Curran, Thomas, and Andrew P. Hill. "Perfectionism Is Increasing Over Time: A Meta-Analysis of Birth Cohort Differences from 1989 to 2016." *Psychological Bulletin* 145, no. 4 (2019): 410–429. https://doi.org/10.1037/bul0000138.

Dalton-Smith, Saundra. *Sacred Rest: Recover Your Life, Renew Your Energy, Restore Your Sanity*. New York: Faithwords, 2017.

Dillard, Annie. *The Writing Life*. New York: Harper Collins, 1989.

Duffy, Chris. "How to Redefine Your Self-Worth (with Meag-gan O'Reilly)." Produced by TED and PRX. *How to Be a Better Person*. March 2021. Podcast. 28:35. https://play.prx.org/listen?ge=prx_357_d20c4a65-8ff7-40d6-b5e6-cfb6112192e6&uf=https%3A%2F%2Ffeeds.feedburner.com%2FHowToBeABetterHuman.

Ferguson, Tamara J., Heidi L. Eyre, and Michael Ashbaker. "Unwanted Identities: A Key Variable in Shame-Anger Links and Gender Differences in Shame." *Sex Roles* 42 (2000): 133–157.

Frankl, Viktor. *Man's Search for Meaning*. Boston: Beacon Press, 2006.

Freudenberger, Herbert J. "Staff Burn-Out." *Journal of Social Issues* 30 (1974): 159–165. https://doi.org/10.1111/j.1540-4560.1974.tb00706.x

Gaudreau, Patrick, Benjamin J. I. Schellenberg, Alexandre Gareau, Kristina Kljajic, and Stéphanie Manoni-Millar. "Because Excellencism Is More Than Good Enough: On the Need to Distinguish the Pursuit of Excellence from the Pursuit of Perfection." *Journal of Personality and Social Psychology* 122, no. 6 (2022): 1117–1145. https://doi.org/10.1037/pspp0000411.

Geyer, Latrina T., Tim Cunningham, Krystyna Rastorguieva, and Chad W. M. Ritenour. "An Abundance Mindset Approach to Support Nurse Well-Being: The Feasibility of Peer Support." *Nurse Leader* 21, no. 4 (August 2023): 489–493. https://doi.org/10.1016/j.mnl.2023.03.013.

References

Hecht, Jennifer M. "On the Strength of All Conviction and the Stamina of Love." In *The Next Ancient World*. North Adams, MA: Tupelo Press, 2001.

International Classification of Diseases. "Burnout." https://icd.who.int /browse11/l-m/en#/http://id.who.int/icd/entity/129180281.

Jansen, Wendy. "Abundance in Positive Design: Part A: The Image of 'Unlimited Good.'" Academia. https://www.academia.edu/184001/Abundance_and _scarcity_thinking_and_Design_of_Organizations_and_Networks.

Jethuri, Kunal. "Pareto Principle: The Law of the Vital Few." Medium, January 26, 2023. https://medium.com/@igniobydigitate/pareto-principle-the-law -of-the-vital-few-e10d3123eea5.

Kalil, Ariel, Susan Mayer, and Rohen Shah. "Scarcity and Inattention." *Becker Friedman Institute for Economics*, no. 2022-76 (June 2023). https://ssrn.com /abstract=4138637.

Kaufman, Scott B. *Transcend: The New Science of Self-Actualization*. New York: TarcherPerigee, 2020.

Kleitman, Nathaniel. "Basic Rest-Activity Cycle—22 Years Later." *Sleep* 5, no. 4 (September 1982): 311–317. https://doi.org/10.1093/sleep/5.4.311.

Kross, Ethan. *Chatter: The Voice in Our Head, Why It Matters, and How to Harness It*. New York: Crown, 2021.

Lang, Martin, Jan Krátký, John H. Shaver, Danijela Jerotijević, and Dimitris Xygalatas. "Effects of Anxiety on Spontaneous Ritualized Behavior." *Current Biology* 25, no. 14 (2015): 1892–1897. https://doi.org/10.1016 /j.cub.2015.05.049.

LeJeune, Jenna, and Jason B. Luoma. *Values in Therapy: A Clinician's Guide to Helping Clients Explore Values, Increase Psychological Flexibility & Live a More Meaningful Life*. Oakland: Context Press, 2019.

Lewallen, Jennifer, and Elizabeth Behm-Morawitz. "Pinterest or Thinterest?: Social Comparison and Body Image on Social Media," *Social Media and Society* 2, no. 1 (2016). https://doi.org/10.1177/2056305116640559.

Madore, Kevin P., and Anthony D. Wagner. "Multicosts of Multitasking." *Cerebrum* (March–April 2019). https://www.ncbi.nlm.nih.gov/pmc/articles /PMC7075496.

Maslow, Abraham H. "A Theory of Human Motivation." *Psychological Review* 50, no. 4 (1943): 370–396. https://doi.org/10.1037/h0054346.

Masters-Waage, Theodore C., Eva Peters, Charis Loo, and Jochen Matthias Reb. "A Scarcity Mindset Reduces Salary Goals through Lowering Employment Self-Efficacy." *Academy of Management Proceedings*, no. 1 (2022). https://doi.org/10.5465/AMBPP.2022.13753abstract.

McMains, Stephanie and Sabine Kastner. "Interactions of Top-Down and Bottom-Up Mechanisms in Human Visual Cortex." *Journal of Neuroscience* 31, no. 2 (2011): 587–597. https://doi.org/10.1523/JNEUROSCI.3766 -10.2011.

Miller, Kaitlyn. "Discussing the Harms of Toxic Productivity with an Expert Psychologist." Grey Journal, 2021, https://greyjournal.net/hustle/grow /discussing-the-harms-of-toxic-productivity-with-an-expert-psychologist.

Morgan, Alice. *What Is Narrative Therapy? An Easy-to-Read Introduction.* Adelaide, SA: Dulwich Centre Publications, 2000.

Moyer, Melinda W. "Your Body Knows You're Burned Out." *The New York Times*. February 15, 2022, https://www.nytimes.com/2022/02/15/well/live /burnout-work-stress.html.

Mullainathan, Sendhil, and Eldar Shafir. *Scarcity: Why Having Too Little Means So Much.* New York: Times Books, 2013.

National Library of Medicine. "Depression: What Is Burnout," Last modified June 18, 2020. https://www.ncbi.nlm.nih.gov/books/NBK279286.

Obama, Michelle. *Becoming.* New York: Crown, 2018.

Odell, Jenny. *How to Do Nothing: Resisting the Attention Economy.* New York: Melville House, 2019.

Orth, Ulrich, and Richard W. Robins. "The Development of Self-Esteem." *Current Directions in Psychological Science* 23, no. 5 (July 2014): 381–387. https://doi.org/10.1177/0963721414547414.

Orth, Ulrich, Ruth Y. Erol, and Eva C. Luciano. "Development of Self-Esteem from Age 4 to 94 Years: A Meta-Analysis of Longitudinal Studies." *Psychological Bulletin* 144, no. 10 (2018): 1045–1080. https://doi.org /10.1037/bul0000161.

Patricolo, Gail Elliott, Amanda LaVoie, Barbara Slavin, Nancy L. Richards, Deborah Jagow, and Karen Armstrong. "Beneficial Effects of Guided Imagery or Clinical Massage on the Status of Patients in a Progressive Care Unit." *Critical Care Nurse* 37, no. 1 (2017): 62-69. https://doi.org/10.4037 /ccn2017282.

Patt, Anthony, and Richard Zeckhauser. "Action Bias and Environmental Decisions." *Journal of Risk and Uncertainty* 21, no. 1 (2000): 45–72. https://doi.org/10.1023/A:1026517309871.

Sandel, Michael J. *The Tyranny of Merit*. New York: Farrar, Straus and Giroux, 2020.

Selva, Joaquin. "Why Shame and Guilt Are Functional for Mental Health." Positive Psychology. January 22, 2018. https://positivepsychology.com /shame-guilt.

Shah, Anuj K., Sendhil Mullainathan, and Eldar Shafir. "Some Consequences of Having Too Little." *Science* 338, no. 682 (2012). https://doi.org/10.1126 /science.1222426.

Sirois, Fushcia M., and Danielle S. Molnar. "Perfectionistic Strivings and Concerns Are Differentially Associated with Self-Rated Health Beyond Negative Affect." *Journal of Research in Personality* 70 (2017): 73–83. https://doi.org/10.1016/j.jrp.2017.06.003.

Smith, Eliot R., Diane M. Mackie, and Heather M. Claypool, *Social Psychology*. 3rd ed. New York: Psychology Press, 2014.

Smith, Martin M., Simon B. Sherry, Samantha Chen, Donald H. Saklofske, Christopher Mushquash, Gordon L. Flett, and Paul L. Hewitt. "The Perniciousness of Perfectionism: A Meta-Analytic Review of the Perfectionism-Suicide Relationship." *Journal of Personality* 86, no. 3 (2018): 522–542. https://doi.org/10.1111/jopy.12333.

Stoeber, Joachim. "The Dual Nature of Perfectionism in Sports: Relationships with Emotion, Motivation, and Performance." *International Review of Sport and Exercise Psychology* 4, no. 2 (2011): 128–145. https://doi.org/10.1080 /1750984X.2011.604789.

Summerville, Amy, and Neal J. Roese. "Dare to Compare: Fact-Based versus Simulation-Based Comparison in Daily Life." *Journal of Experimental Social Psychology* 44, no. 3 (2008): 664–671. https://doi.org/10.1016 /j.jesp.2007.04.002.

Tangney, June P., Jeffrey Stuewig, and Andres G. Martinez. "Two Faces of Shame: Understanding Shame and Guilt in the Prediction of Jail Inmates' Recidivism." *Psychological Science* 25, no. 3 (2014): 799–805. https://doi.org/10.1177/0956797613508790.

Tawwab, Nedra G. *Set Boundaries, Find Peace: A Guide to Reclaiming Yourself.* New York: TarcherPerigee, 2021.

Tracy, Jessica L., and Richard W. Robins. "Putting the Self Into Self-Conscious Emotions: A Theoretical Model." *Psychological Inquiry* 15, no. 2 (2004): 103–125. https://ubc-emotionlab.ca/wp-content/files_mf /publishedtargetarticle.pdf.

Wallace, David F. "*This Is Water* by David Foster Wallace." Farnam Street. https://fs.blog/david-foster-wallace-this-is-water.

Zanto, Theodore P., and Adam Gazzaley. "Aging of the Frontal Lobe." *Handbook of Clinical Neurology* 163 (2019): 369–389. https://doi.org/10.1016/B978-0 -12-804281-6.00020-3.

Zhao, Jiaying, and Brandon M. Tomm. "Psychological Responses to Scarcity." *Oxford Research Encyclopedias*. February 26, 2018. https://doi.org /10.1093/acrefore/9780190236557.013.41.

Acknowledgments

"I come as one, but I stand as ten thousand."

—Maya Angelou, "Our Grandmothers"

The process of writing this book has been one of my greatest endeavors, filled with uncertainties, joy, and a lot of hard work. None of which would have been possible without the support of my community—the people I'd like to thank here.

There would be no book without my family. My loving parents, Tahzeeb and Nasir, who not only *literally* taught me how to read and write—but who also cultivated my skills, nurtured my curiosity about literature and the world, supported all of my choices, gave me the safe space to think critically and find my voice—and are my strongest safeguards. I am fearless to fly high because I trust they will be there to catch my fall—and for that, I am infinitely grateful.

Our siblings are our longest relationships, and I can't imagine my life without mine. Thank you to my younger sister, Sundus, for being my soulmate—my partner in everything I do, the sounding board for all my life's decisions, for being there to support me in everything I do wholeheartedly, and for choosing all my outfits (ha!). For my brother, Suhaib—having an older brother who always took me alongside his adventures helped me develop so many of the values and confidence that I am proud of today—thank you for being my first friend and teaching me to be unapologetically authentic.

And to the final piece of my family—Feraz. Being married to a writer is challenging; so much time, attention and energy go into creating something. What's special about you is that you welcomed and celebrated the challenge. I am lucky to have a partner who patiently and excitedly made space for this writing journey in our lives; whose gentle encouragement, humor, and generosity in spirit has consistently helped me through many difficult moments (while writing this book, and in general life). Like seahorses who pair together in the vast ocean and remain anchored to each other amid the currents, I am deeply thankful to be anchored to you through the currents of our life.

They say it takes a village to raise a child; I say, it also takes a village to sustain an adult. Our "village" is powerful; a strong community helps us feel a sense of belonging, acceptance, and love. My community is an indispensable part of my life—friends who became family, and who celebrated every joy and mourned every loss with me. I want to dedicate a moment to appreciate Chowdhury Aunty and Shaghufta Aunty, who are no longer with us. Your love and kindness toward me and my family showed me what the incredible supportive power of community and sisterhood look like. Even though you might not have intended it, you left an indelible mark on my life. To Naseem Aunty and the Sabir family, as well as Ruhee, I have profound gratitude for your continuous compassion, generosity, presence, and midnight birthday cakes. And finally, to my "inner circle of trust"—Mali, Baber, Jessica, and Rachana: you keep me grounded and forever connected to my roots; I wouldn't want to live life without you in my corner.

I'm hoping that through some marvel of fate, this book lands in the hands of two influential high school English teachers at George S. Henry Academy: Mrs. Wolfson and Mr. Gibson. Wherever you are,

I want you to know that your support in encouraging me to express my ideas through writing, especially when I was so young, helped me believe that I could be a writer one day too.

A lot of this book is rooted in scientific research on psychology and sociology. I have depended on many other writers and academics to enlighten me as I wrote out my own thoughts on this subject. To all the authors, researchers, and clinicians who have devoted their lives to helping us learn more and expand the reach of the field of psychology—we are all indebted to you.

To close, I want to thank the people who made this book into a reality—the incredible team at PESI Publishing for taking a chance on a debut writer. Karsyn Morse, for reaching out to me initially with an idea for a book. Kayla Church and Kate Sample, for working tirelessly with me, responding to all my emails, answering all my questions, and quelling all my anxieties. And of course, Chelsea Thompson, for editing my work numerous times over two years, helping clarify my thoughts, and for offering insights, suggestions, and guidance with patience, honesty, and grace.

And most importantly I want to thank you, the reader who picked up this book. Wherever you are in your journey, I am humbled that you let me be a small part of it.

This is a big moment for me—I am the first in my family of migrants and immigrants to publish a book. For a family who experienced two wars and displacement, moved to live in three different countries, and consistently had to leave something behind, this allows me to add to my family's legacy—to pass forward something that did not exist before.

About the Author

Israa Nasir, MHC-LP, is a New York City based psychotherapist, writer, and the founder of WellGuide—a digital community for mental health awareness. Her work is centered on transforming the way we talk about mental health, taking it from a place of shame to a place of empowerment. A Pakistani-Canadian child of immigrants, she has a specific focus on mental health, identity formation, and healing for the AAPI immigrant (first and second generation) community. Israa has been featured in NBC, *Vox*, *HuffPost*, *Teen Vogue*, and other major publications and been invited to speak at corporations such as Google, Meta, and Yale.